It requires courage to be honest, but it also requires skill. Drs. Donoghue and Siegel teach in a deeply human way the skills needed to communicate with genuine love.

**Archbishop Desmond Tutu**
Author of *Made for Goodness*

The face of our world can be positively transformed by learning but a few new communication skills—this book is brimming with them! It is like having kind, yet clear, mentors present to help make all of our relationships even better.

**Robert J. Wicks**
Author of *Riding the Dragon*

I can definitely see this book being used as a tool to guide warriors and their loved ones in building bridges of communication in their relationships and with their families.

**Chaplain (Lt. Col.) Ron Martin-Minnich**
Army National Guard

Donoghue and Siegel inform and guide with sparkling wit and genuine wisdom. For people who want to love and be loved, this is the book to read.

**Ed Waggoner**
Yale Divinity School

I recommend *We Really Need to Talk* to anyone interested in improving work or personal relationships—at work to increase clarity, efficiency, and effectiveness in accomplishing goals and at home for anyone hoping to enrich close relationships with lasting trust and intimacy.

**Kim Fairey**
Director of Advancement
Horizons National

I am a clinical social worker and am always seeking resources on interpersonal communication. I have not read a book in recent memory that is as straightforward, comprehensive, and clear as *We Really Need to Talk*. I know it will be helpful to professionals, families, and couples. This is a very special book.

**Don Marshall**
Executive Director
The Charlton School

# contents

## Part Three: **talk this way**

# acknowledgments

We owe sincerest thanks to many people who helped to make this book possible. First of all, we are greatly indebted to our clients who over the years have trusted us and talked openly and courageously about their deepest concerns.

We thank our dear friends John Balistreri and Carol Look. We are indebted to John for his labor of love, being with us each step of the book's development and for reading and rereading the manuscript, and to Carol for her insight and eagle eye.

We are very grateful to Jacob A. Clement, CH (CPT) and Jeffrey T. Haugh, MC, (COL) who generously gave of their time to tell us their fascinating story and to guide us in writing about military matters.

We extend our profound gratitude to The Very Reverend Robert V. Taylor for his loving, magnanimous support.

We are humbled by the gracious comments of the very busy individuals who willingly read the manuscript and offered their responses to it, which are printed at the front of the book.

Finally, our thanks to the dedicated professionals at Sorin Books for bringing this book to print, especially to our editor, Susanna Q. Cover, for her skilled and talented work.

# we really need
# to talk

Chapter One

# *everyone needs to talk*

The single biggest problem in communication
is the illusion that it has taken place.

—George Bernard Shaw

"We need to talk," George Costanza on Seinfeld moaned.
"These are the worst four words in the English language." For
George they are datespeak for "I need to break things off" or "I
like you, but . . ." Like George, many people hear these words as
the dreaded precursor to the end of a relationship. For others,
the words spell the end of a job. The phrase is similar in foreboding to "step into my office," a possible preamble to "you're
fired." For most people, the words "we need to talk" spell trouble. For a teenager, these words might trigger fear that parents
have found something in the bedroom or gotten a call from a
school principal. A husband could worry that his wife may have
discovered disturbing sites on his computer. A wife hearing "we
need to talk" might be alarmed that her husband has seen the
real estate brochures. "We need to talk" isn't heard as an invitation to discuss. Too often it means, "I'm going to talk and you're
going to listen and change."

Despite their pejorative reputation, the words "we need to talk" don't always mean a breakup or a dismissal or a threat. We *do* need to talk. We need to talk almost as much as we need to breathe. "Fish gotta swim. Birds gotta fly." We gotta talk. There are many, many reasons why we have to talk.

## We Need to Talk to
## Know Ourselves and Be Known by Others

Possibly the central reasons we talk are to come to know ourselves and to make ourselves known to others. Babies cry, whimper, howl, gurgle, and hum. Sometimes they make sounds because they are wet or hungry. At other times they just seem to want to hear themselves, one of their first forays into self-awareness. The need to know themselves and to be known by others is one of the reasons teenagers talk to one another by the hour in person, on the phone, and by every other means the latest technologies provide. When Mia talks, she is hearing herself, her thoughts, views, feelings, beliefs, attitudes, and what she values, fears, and hopes. Who Mia is and what she stands for come into focus as she talks. She gets to know herself by putting herself into words. She also meets her need to be known to her friend who is listening. Mia discovers herself by speaking out loud. Sarah meets her own need to be known to herself by "talking" into her journal or diary. Being more introverted than Mia, Sarah clarifies her thoughts and values in private before expressing herself in public. Both grow to know themselves by talking to themselves or to others.

> We need to talk almost as much as we need to breathe. "Fish gotta swim. Birds gotta fly." We gotta talk.

Teenagers are not the only ones who come to know themselves by listening to themselves speak. One of the primary reasons for talking is self-discovery. We need to voice who we are to know who we are. "Out of the fullness of the heart the mouth speaketh" (Mt 12:34). We know the secrets of our heart by voicing them. Self-discovery comes from honest revelation. Only by admitting what you truly feel, think, and value can you know yourself. Growth in self-knowledge requires that you be freely honest with yourself.

When you are transparent to yourself, you allow yourself to acknowledge and articulate whatever is happening within you—vague thoughts, troublesome feelings, delights, yearnings, questions, dreams, hopes, and fears. You come to know yourself by reflecting on what you are recognizing within yourself. You learn not to fear yourself by naming what previously had not been admitted. By being transparent with another, you put yourself into words in front of yourself and in the process see yourself more clearly.

> Only by admitting what you truly feel, think, and value can you know yourself.

Laura, for example, came to know herself more deeply by sharing her troubled feelings in a counseling session with us. Laura is a lovely mother of three teenage daughters. She needed to talk because, as she says:

> I was married once before when I was very young. His name was Kevin. I was only seventeen and it lasted only six months and then I never saw him again. It was a stupid thing we did. A couple of days ago an old friend of mine happened to mention that Kevin died last year. I felt so sad. It seemed weird. Why was I so upset when I had hardly even thought about him all this time? It feels so freeing to talk to you about it. I guess I just needed to talk it through so that I could understand myself and sort it out.

Talking allowed Laura an opportunity to explore confusing feelings of sadness that were upsetting her. Like Laura, you have feelings that can be a relief to voice and can provide insight into yourself. You might have unpleasant feelings in the presence of a certain man or woman or when you are in a particular kind of situation or group. If you know your body's signals, you might recognize feelings of unease or stress, when you perspire, stutter, or get a headache or backache. Allow yourself to verbalize what you are feeling: envy, inferiority, sexual attraction, anger, resentment. By stating the feelings to yourself or to an empathic, non-judgmental listener, you can free yourself from the stress of these feelings as well as from the hidden guilt or shame that they can induce. Identifying and accepting feelings can help you to know yourself as well as accept yourself. You need to talk openly and honestly to know yourself, be yourself, and like yourself.

Being known is as primal a need as being loved. One way to satisfy your need to be known is by disclosing yourself in words to someone else. Ironically, as desirable as it is to be known, it can be frightening to reveal yourself. So instead of using words to reveal yourself, you might be inclined to use them to disguise yourself. You could, for example, use words to boast or exaggerate when you really feel insecure. Or you may tease or joke when actually you are angry. Sometimes you might reveal part of what you are feeling; for example, you might admit to slight hurt, when the truth is that you are devastated. A friend said to us, "I admit I was a little bit hurt when my son Edward said he wouldn't be coming for Christmas." The fact that she refused to talk to him for the next six months suggests that our friend was more than "a little bit" hurt. A French cynic remarked, "Words were invented to keep people apart." The philosopher Friedrich Nietzsche expressed a similar sentiment: "Talking much about oneself may be a way of hiding oneself." Singer Joe South lamented the disingenuousness of people's words in his song, "Games People Play."

> Oh the games people play now, every night and every day now.
> Never meaning what they say now, never saying what they mean.

In order to be known to your spouse, friend, or child, you have to identify all of the ways that you hide yourself by using or avoiding words. Then you have to admit your feelings to yourself and risk sharing them truthfully. You will need courage to be honest, and you will need to learn the skills for direct, verbal self-disclosure.

## We Need to Talk to Ask for Help

We need to talk in order to have our needs met. Ken's mother is beside herself. "He simply will not speak to his teacher and ask for help," she told us. "I know he won't speak up in class and ask a question, but he won't ask the teacher privately either." Ken is like many of us; we need help, but out of fear or ignorance or embarrassment we will not voice our need. A couple arrived late for their first marriage counseling session. Terry was irate. "He would not stop and ask for directions." Then she turned to her husband and said, "What is wrong with you?"

What is wrong with all of us who are reluctant to voice our needs? Eileen, a beleaguered mother of two teenagers, complained to us that she had "had it!" "I work full time, do all the cooking, and keep a neat house. I do everything. Nobody helps. I just want to leave it all." Through several therapy sessions, Eileen identified her pattern of taking on too many of the responsibilities in the house and then becoming resentful and critical. She realized how powerless she had become with her husband and children while becoming increasingly filled with rage and self-pity. She hadn't recognized that, though she had these feelings for a long time, she had not voiced them. Gradually she learned to express her needs for help from her husband and from her boys. She backed away from her role of supermom-martyr-critic, made herself far less available, and relinquished many household tasks. She found that by meeting her own needs for rest and for time to be with her friends and by voicing her expectations, she became calmer and more assertive.

A construction foreman learned a similar lesson about the necessity of asserting one's needs. He came to see us when he began to suffer anxiety attacks. At work, fearful of confrontation with his employees, he resisted telling them when they were out of line or when their work was unacceptable. His anxiety was the result of repressed anger and resentment and a horrible sense of being overwhelmed and helpless. When he learned to express his need for his employees to complete their tasks responsibly, his anxiety lifted.

Parents fail to state their needs for respect and cooperation, and spouses their need for attention and appreciation. Friends can refuse to ask for help; family members can be reticent to make known their needs, yet be hurt when no one steps up to provide support. A sad elderly man admitted, "I never knew how much I needed to hear my brother ask if he could help me move until he offered." Many people are afraid to voice their needs for fear of rejection. And when they try, often they do not know how to make their needs known without resorting to blame or judgment or attack. You have to be honest about your needs, admit them to yourself, and learn to express them constructively to others.

## We Need to Talk to Provide Information and Direction

We need to talk to convey information. We talk to a mechanic to explain the problems with our car, the doctor to describe our symptoms of pain, the waitress to place our order. It sounds basic, doesn't it, until you hear the frustration of the mechanic about the inaccurate description the car owner gave of the problem, the dismay of the doctor regarding the omissions and lack of clarity in the patient's complaints, and the impatience of the waitress: "He claims he ordered the steak rare, but I know he didn't." Often, information is conveyed inaccurately, in a misleading way, or not at all. Recently, we wasted time looking for pickles in the wrong aisle of a supermarket, thanks to three store clerks offering inaccurate information. And we have driven miles out of our way following a taxi driver's directions that were just plain wrong.

When you provide information, you have a responsibility to be clear and accurate. The store clerks would have been more helpful by telling the truth: "I don't know." The same may be said for the taxi driver giving directions. We read with amusement an article that discussed cultural differences in giving directions. In Iraq it is considered offensive to respond, "I don't know," when asked directions. The person asked will suggest any route regardless of its accuracy. Better to be wrong than to offend seems to be the guiding principle.

We all respect the person who is careful to articulate helpful information. We have our favorite columnist, news anchor, or reporter who helps us to make sense of events. The priest, imam, rabbi, or minister who preaches scripture making it clearly relevant to our lives is a godsend. We recall with profound appreciation the cherished history or science teacher who made the subject not only interesting but meaningful.

Parents face daily the responsibility of imparting information to the endless "whys" of a toddler and to the curious minds of developing adolescents. Recently, a mother told us of her joy in informing her daughter about sex:

> I was not looking forward to the conversation; neither was Sonia. But she was so sweet and asked such good questions. I told her all about her body and what her period will be like. She didn't go "yuck" but instead was really interested. Right at the end though she said, "Don't tell me about the car in the garage stuff. OK?"

Managers have a particular task in talking about their needs and expectations to their staff members. But many managers who are under pressure to complete their own work or who simply lack communication skills fail to express their needs directly. A frustrated sales rep at a large technology firm complained in a coaching session,

> I'm at my wits' end. My boss never tells me clearly what he expects from me. I know he must need me to perform in certain ways, but he won't let me know. I ask for direction and feedback, but I get nowhere. He's the worst manager I've ever had. I don't think he wants me to succeed.

We have heard similar complaints from some nurses. They start their shifts with unclear messages from their supervisors and then endure a doctor's rage when he is upset that his orders were not followed. Spouses are exasperated at being criticized for not satisfying needs that they were supposed to have known without being told. Managers, teachers, and parents need to be clear about their expectations. It helps to get feedback that expectations have been understood. A waitress repeating an order probably has learned from experience the value of confirming what she has heard from the customer. If you are frustrated that others are not meeting your expectations or satisfying your needs, ask yourself, "Did I provide all the necessary information? How clearly did I state what I wanted?"

## We Need to Talk to Find Relief

Kate sat opposite us crying, then smiling weakly, then crying again. Finally, she breathed deeply.

I'm so relieved to be talking about this. I know it happened a long time ago, but I've never talked about it. When it happened I knew I couldn't. My parents, especially my mother, would have blamed me, like I led him on. I was only sixteen. I think I felt afraid of my sexuality ever since. I think it's why I'm overweight—to keep guys away.

Kate was telling us about her high school English teacher who had fondled her repeatedly. She described her fear, confusion, and guilt. For fifteen years she had kept the incident inside, where it had shaped her sense of herself and her body.

Victims of rape and sexual abuse frequently endure shame and self-loathing—feelings that fester in intensity the longer the events are held secret. You surely have had experiences and feelings that have become distorted from not being spoken and explored in the presence of a listener. You may view yourself as evil or sick because of some sexual behavior as a child with a sibling, or with an eighth grader of your own sex at camp. You may have concluded that you are a loser or helpless due to your parents' repeated remarks, "You are helpless; here let me do that." You can feel afraid of trying anything new and have no idea why. Freud speaks of relief from the consequences of these critical and distorted attitudes toward ourselves when he describes the "talking cure," the mysterious alleviation of symptoms such as depression and aggression as a result of talking openly. As the novelist Marcel Proust puts it, "We are healed of a suffering only by expressing it to the full." Psychic pain is frequently relieved by nothing more than revealing one's experiences and feelings to another.

Psychotherapy, whatever its method, is based on the effectiveness of talk therapy. Over and over clients have concluded a session saying, "I feel so much better. Thank you." Yet they have done the talking. Their improved spirits owe much less to the therapist's advice or analysis than to their own articulation of their life events, their thoughts, and their emotions to someone who doesn't impede or burden them with judgments or blame. You can find this kind of relief with a friend, parent, or relative. It doesn't have to be a professional who listens. A somber woman mourning the loss of her recently deceased sister told us, "What I will miss most was that I could tell Adrian anything. She never judged. I always knew that she understood and loved me."

> Psychic pain is frequently relieved by nothing more than revealing one's experiences and feelings to another.

The potential for relief from the burden of guilt and, according to Cardinal Francis Stafford, "the opportunity for people to reflect profoundly on their interior life," inspired the Catholic Church to revive attention to the sacrament of reconciliation in January 2009. The confessional experience can be an enormous source of comfort and release of guilt, especially when the person confessing believes that the priest is a conduit to God's love and acceptance. The experience suffers when the priest judges rather than forgives, a frequent enough occurrence that might explain the sacrament's decline.

A *60 Minutes* episode portrayed a dramatic example of the need to talk in order to experience relief from guilt. Rape victim Jennifer Thompson's eyewitness identification of her rapist sent Ronald Cotton to jail for life. When another prisoner, Bobby Poole, confessed to a fellow inmate that he had committed the rape, Cotton was awarded a second trial. Jennifer, however, dismissed Poole's admission and asserted that she remembered unequivocally that Cotton was the perpetrator. Cotton was reconvicted and sent back to prison. Only when DNA evidence exonerated Cotton and proved Poole's guilt was Ronald Cotton freed. He had spent eleven years of his life in jail on the basis of Jennifer's identification.

Jennifer was tormented with overwhelming guilt that her error had resulted in such crushing consequences to an innocent man. She needed to talk, and Ronald Cotton was willing to listen. Jennifer told him, "If I apologize every minute of every day, it would not express the depth of my regret." She said later, "When Ronald took my hand and said, 'I forgive you,' a terrible weight lifted from me." Today Ronald has a wife and child who are friends with Jennifer's family. Ronald and Jennifer lecture together to police and attorneys on the dangers of false memory and eyewitness identification. Their need to talk no longer is to find relief but to instruct.

## We Need to Talk to Connect

No man is an island, nor is a woman or a child. At no other time in history has it been so evident that people want to talk to one another. Technological means of "talking" have exploded in popularity. Most people talk many times a day on their cell phones. Individuals Twitter, text, instant message, blog, go to chat rooms, e-mail, and log on to Facebook, LinkedIn, or MySpace in a seemingly insatiable need to connect and to communicate.

As consultants and lecturers, we spend a lot of time in airports and on planes. Often we are amused by the sight of people walking along, talking animatedly on a Bluetooth. Sometimes it takes us a minute to realize that they are not talking to themselves. (We have heard stories of freshmen in college and insecure folks of all ages talking into a dead phone so as to appear popular or important.) It is striking how many people whip out their cell phones as soon as a plane lands. Travel on Amtrak now requires earplugs or a seat in the quiet car to escape the sound of voices talking loudly into phones. Frequently, we are frustrated by passengers seated near us on planes and trains who seem to need to talk loudly to total strangers for an entire trip.

The need to tell *you* about *me* is apparently very compelling even if the degree of connection is minimal or even risky. People over-disclose on Facebook, signing up in huge numbers to reveal their thoughts and divulge their preferences or prejudices. While the information is sent out into a galaxy composed of millions of strangers, people extract from the experience a sense of membership in a community, however loosely linked. More and more social commentators wonder, though, if the relationships developed in these networks ever evolve into intimacy.

Talking is an essential part of connecting and of forming community. In a discussion about the Great Depression, Walter Kirn noted in his article "What's a Depression, Daddy?" that the economic disaster "had a two-fold effect" on his grandfather's family and friends: "It laid them low financially while drawing them closer personally. The agent of this coziness was language." People in England who lived through the Blitz describe the community formed in the bomb shelters where they began calling one another "love" and "dear" and "pet."

These examples of people drawing closer in a time of calamity demonstrate the swell of comfort that is derived from talking. You tell someone your woe; they tell you theirs. Nothing changes. You still have lost your job or your savings, but you do feel better. You are not alone; you are connected. John Montone, roving reporter for WINS radio, encourages listeners to call in and narrate the things about which they want to "moan and groan." He concludes their call saying, "Don't you feel better?"

Talking to connect certainly is not restricted to sharing troubles. We share stories of all kinds: golf stories, fish stories, tall tales, personal experiences, family happenings, our successes and failures and those of our children. We tell funny stories. We pass jokes along on the Internet, and most of us can't resist telling the one that we just heard and find knee-slappingly funny. We tease and engage in light-hearted banter. At times we interact with others in chitchat and small talk. We are social beings and we talk to socialize.

Exclusion from social contact has been an age-old method of punishment. In the Middle Ages, banishment from one's city was a dreaded penalty for certain crimes. Today, the guilty pay for their crimes in prison, where the worst punishment is solitary confinement. Such isolation from society is not only painful but it also endangers mental health. We need social contact not only for pleasure but for sanity. A psychologist from the University of California, Craig Haney, studied a hundred inmates at Pelican Bay State Prison. He found that prisoners who spend months in complete isolation "begin to lose the ability to initiate behavior of any kind. Chronic apathy, lethargy, depression, and despair often result."

## We Need to Talk, but Not Too Much or Too Little

You may not recall being taught "rules" of disclosure, but you and all of society operate on unstated notions of the appropriateness or inappropriateness of revealing yourself. You know by the time that you are in first grade that there are some things you shouldn't say to strangers or should say only within the family; there are times when you should be quiet and other times when your teachers, parents, and friends want to hear from you. You learn from explicit and implicit lessons, by trial and error, and eventually develop a sense of what society deems appropriate self-expression.

*We need social contact not only for pleasure but for sanity.*

Appropriate disclosure of yourself begins a process that leads to trust and connection with another person. The ogre Shrek from the motion picture *Shrek* compares this process of gradual self-revelation to peeling away the layers of an onion. When you first meet someone and begin to talk, you remove the first layer by saying something impersonal and uncontroversial, such as, "Isn't this a beautiful spring day?" or, "The highway was congested this morning." When this first comment is received and reciprocated, you remove your next layer of self by speaking of something slightly more revealing; for example, "I wish I could get out more on a spring day. I work in an office." You reveal more layers as the conversation or relationship deepens. It is inappropriate disclosure if you share too deeply too quickly; for example, if you start right out with "My boss doesn't know it, but when he travels I take two- or three-hour lunches." Sharing yourself too deeply before you have progressed through the superficial "onion layers" confuses and sometimes frightens the other person. It strains or breaks trust.

If, however, your sharing and the other's sharing remain on the outer layers and never advance, the degree of connection will remain static. Sometimes such a level might satisfy your mutual needs. Interactions with the letter carrier, for example, represent such an exchange. Yet if you need a profound connection, then continued surface sharing will frustrate and disappoint you. Many relationships become and remain dissatisfying when one or both of the members fail to reveal deeper layers of themselves. Parents complain that their children don't talk about what they are thinking or what they have been doing. Spouses feel loneliness when their partners do not share what they are experiencing or feeling. Sadly, relationships that could be far more intimate remain starved of personal sharing because one or both partners are afraid.

> Fear usually causes inadequate disclosure: fear of being hurt or misunderstood, fear of sounding weak or foolish, fear of being judged.

Fear usually causes inadequate disclosure: fear of being hurt or misunderstood, fear of sounding weak or foolish, fear of being judged. People who are lonely often perpetuate that loneliness because of such fears. They resist going deeper "into the onion," preventing their relationships from developing toward intimacy. Ironically, a desire for closeness or a desperate need to have a friend can sometimes provoke a person to over-disclose, to blurt out information that should be reserved for a more developed relationship. We rely on social cues to subtly dictate the pace of disclosure, and we need to recognize within ourselves the feelings that may impede that recognition. Failure to do so leads to behaviors of sharing too much or too little, which may result in loneliness.

## We Need to Talk to Voice Support, Encouragement, and Love

We need to talk not only to satisfy our needs but also to fulfill the needs of others. They, like us, yearn to be supported, affirmed, and encouraged. The philosopher Martin Buber states this truth in his book *I and Thou*:

> Man wishes to be confirmed in his being by men and wishes to have a presence in the being of the other. . . . Secretly and bashfully he watches for a YES which allows him to be and which can come to him only from one human person to

another. It is from one another that the heavenly bread of self-being is passed.

One way to express that *yes*, that full affirmation, is by words: "Well done!" "I respect the way you handled that," "I admire the way you raise your children," "Thank you for a wonderful meal." These words express a positive attitude toward another. The ultimate in such verbal affirmation is "I love you." You raise the spirits of someone you care for with words of encouragement, respect, and appreciation. But too frequently these words go unspoken. When we consult with corporations, the employees often voice their reluctance to compliment the quality work of their colleagues. They fear looking insincere or manipulative. "I'm afraid he'd be thinking, what's he after?" is the way one vice president put it. Yet time and again when these workers risk verbalizing their affirmation of a colleague, they note afterwards how satisfying the encounter was. One person said, "It was quite pleasing, actually. She was doing a superb job and very much appreciated my remarks." He added with a warm laugh, "Probably should do a bit more of that at home."

The most effective managers are free to offer authentic praise. So are the most growth-prompting teachers and parents. Spouses who are closest express their love most openly. Other partners in strained relationships grow desperate for words of thanks and esteem from each other. A lovely but sad woman confessed to us, "He never notices what I wear, let alone compliments me. I think he loves me but doesn't want to show it." Parents, too, can be amiss in not praising their children, whether for fear of spoiling them or simply out of awkwardness. The great cellist Pablo Casals advocated unstinting affirmation.

> Each second we live is a new and unique moment of the universe, a moment that never was before and never will be again. And what do we teach our children in school? We teach them that two and two make four and that Paris is the capital of France. When will we also teach them what they are? We should say to each of them: Do you know what you are? You are a marvel. You are unique. In all of the world there is no other child like you. And look at your body—

what a wonder it is! Your legs, your arms, your cunning fingers, the way you move! You may become a Shakespeare, a Michelangelo, a Beethoven. You have the capacity for anything. Yes, you are a marvel. And when you grow up, can you then harm another who is, like you, a marvel? You must cherish one another. You must work—we must all work—to make this world worthy of its children.

You can withhold your words of love and support, but in doing so you deprive yourself of joy while you starve the other of your affection. Becoming more free to express your respect, your appreciation, and your love means becoming more whole and more alive while giving life and hope to others.

## We Need to Talk in Order to Correct and Confront

Bono, of the rock group U2, made a phone call to Greg Kot, the music critic of the *Chicago Tribune*, after Kot had written disapprovingly of the band. Bono said, "You've offended us. . . . There's a dark cloud over us and we need to talk." No matter how famous or established, Bono needed to be understood, and he needed to correct what he believed were unfair judgments. He needed to talk and wasn't stopped by fear of looking petty or by fear of the critic's reprisal.

Each day, as therapists and executive coaches, we listen to individuals who are frustrated, hurt, or furious at someone at work or at home, but, unlike Bono, they let fear stop them from speaking up. Wendy is a smart suburban mother of two little girls. Her husband, Jim, works exhausting hours in New York. He leaves home by 6:00 a.m. and seldom returns before 8:00 p.m. On weekends he sleeps late, naps frequently, and has little contact with his children and wife. Wendy nags a bit

> Peace at all costs rarely results in peace and more likely results in costs more severe than imagined.

and defends herself against Jim's complaints of lack of sex. Yet when we coached her to express herself strongly and clearly in a determined manner, she resisted, saying, "I'm afraid he'd leave me." Fear trumped honesty, and they have continued to live separate, unhappy lives.

Walt is a successful physician who complains that he and his wife live as though they are poor. "We don't go on vacations. We used to ski but we haven't in years. We save because she won't spend." Walt needs to talk but does not do it. "I don't want to hear her cracks like, 'It's always about Walt.' I think I'm afraid of blowing up at her." Fear of her and fear of himself keeps Walt quiet, miserable, and resentful. Fear of confrontation stymies many spouses from expressing their needs, concerns, and feelings.

Fear of confrontation is common in all relationships. Bosses and managers say nothing when an employee takes too many days off or drinks too much at company events. Parents deny telltale signs of a daughter smoking pot. Spouses keep silent when a partner's spending is hurting the family finances. Patients don't speak up when kept waiting an hour in the doctor's office. "Don't rock the boat." "Saying something would only make it worse." "Let's just have peace." These expressions justify saying nothing while allowing destructive behavior to persist. Peace at all costs rarely results in peace and more likely results in costs more severe than imagined.

The following chapters demonstrate the need for talk in key relationships: spouses and partners, parents and children, friendships, as well as business and professional relationships. Part 2 of the book discusses some of the most common ways of talking that fail to bring about satisfying meetings. Part 3 spells out, in a step-by-step fashion, the skills of clear, honest, and effective self-expression.

■ FOR REFLECTION ■

1. What needs do you have that you consider essential to share with the key person in your life?

2. Can you describe a time when you found relief by talking about an event or sharing a feeling?

3. What does "connecting" with someone mean to you? Who are the people in your life with whom it is pleasing to connect? Do you know why?

4. When was the last time you directly affirmed someone?

5. When are you comfortable confronting someone?

Chapter Two

# *talking between*
# *spouses and partners*

"I feel I don't know you at all," she said.
"You've always been so distant. It is so hard to
know you, you let me see so little of you. I still
feel that we are not close to each other.

"I want this to change. I want you to listen to
me."

"Do you want anything?" he asked.

She smiled and shook her head. "We have to
talk," she said.

—Colm Toibin, *The Heather Blazing*

## We Need to Talk to Our Partner

Your central relationship is just that—central. In this relationship
more than any other, effective communication is essential to achieving real connection. If you can speak freely in this relationship,
trusting that you will be understood, and if your partner is fully

Your partner or spouse is like a mirror into which you look to see if you are attractive or interesting, good or bad.

open with you, the rewards are enormous. All the trials of life seem manageable. You don't feel alone. You have someone who understands you, knows you, and wants to hear all that goes on inside you. Can you do the same for your partner? It is precisely because this relationship has such deep meaning to your life that if you are not free to talk, if you are not understood, then no matter what else in your life is good, your self-esteem and *joie de vivre* are seriously threatened.

"I can handle all the pressure at work; it's the tension at home that wrecks me." Tamara is CEO of an international design company. She manages a company with thousands of employees and a budget of hundreds of millions of dollars. "The people, the challenges, the decisions . . . I thrive on all of it. But the stuff with my husband, Geoff, does me in. Sometime he is bitingly critical and sarcastic. He knows just how to hurt me."

Tamara is not unique in finding more stress in her central relationship than in her demanding work. With your partner or spouse, your needs are intense and personal and so your emotions are raw and profound. With the one you love, you most need to be known, loved, and accepted. Tamara's board of directors backs her, and her staff reveres her, but if Geoff is distant or disapproving, her world shakes.

Your partner or spouse is like a mirror into which you look to see if you are attractive or interesting, good or bad. Other people who serve as mirrors for you, such as colleagues at work or members of your church or club, may reflect you in ways that are flattering or critical, but you might discount them. You might think that they really don't know you. They can seem like old-time carnival mirrors that reflect you as too big or too small, but your partner's mirror is the one you look to for an image of who you *really* are. When Elizabeth Barrett looked into the mirror of her family, she saw herself as a delicate, frail young woman who needed to be guarded and shielded from overexertion. When Robert Browning burst into her hothouse world, he became a mirror in which she saw herself as fascinating, beautiful, and desirable. He was a revelation to her of her deepest self. She responded by coming alive to her senses and her talent. In this surge of energetic self-discovery, she needed to talk, to release herself in poetry, and to express to Robert Browning the fullness of her love. She writes of Browning revealing to her a whole new way of looking at life and at herself:

> The face of all the world is changed, I think,
> Since first I heard the footsteps of thy soul
> Move still, oh, still beside me, as they stole
> Betwixt me and the dreadful outer brink
> Of obvious death, where I, who thought to sink,
> Was caught up into love, and taught the whole
> Of life in a new rhythm.
>
> —Sonnet VII

And in her most famous sonnet she bursts with her need to share the feelings inundating her:

> How do I love thee? Let me count the ways.
> I love thee to the depth and breadth and height
> My soul can reach, when feeling out of sight
> For the ends of Being and ideal Grace.
> I love thee to the level of everyday's
> Most quiet need, by sun and candlelight. . . .
>
> —Sonnet XLII

You give to your partner enormous power to define you to yourself. Through him or her you can learn to overcome the inherent self-doubt that threatens you like it threatens everyone. You can learn to risk because, with your partner's love, failure will not destroy your sense of self. The poet E. E. Cummings in his poem "somewhere I have never traveled" describes a lover's liberating touch:

> your slightest look easily will unclose me
> though I have closed myself as fingers
> you open always petal by petal myself as spring
> opens (touching skillfully, mysteriously) her first rose.

You can learn to explore, to change, and to discover new dimensions of yourself. Safe at home, known and loved, you can find your truest voice to express who you really are in all manner of ways and in all types of settings.

Unfortunately, that same power can be a hostile force, crushing your self-esteem and threatening your ability to be freely authentic. Maya is in her late twenties and has been married nine years to her high school sweetheart. She narrated to us the sad story of life with Michael:

> I have totally shut down. I don't respond to my friends' calls. I'm not seeing my family. Michael hasn't worked in two years. He is so angry. He seems jealous of my work and is on me about everything. He says I've gotten flabby. He doesn't like what I wear. He criticizes how I am with our three-year-old. He doesn't want to go out. I don't think he even likes me.

Maya needs to talk, to challenge Michael, to express her hurt as well as her resentment. Michael needs to talk, but not trash talk and not words of criticism that stem from his sense of failure. He needs to speak honestly of his feelings of inadequacy at not working and to listen to Maya's encouragement. They both need to talk—honestly—to one another.

You serve as a mirror for your spouse. What image of him or her are you reflecting? How is your partner seeing herself if you refuse to go out with her socially or to her business functions? How does he see himself when you are impatient with his driving, critical of the way he speaks, unresponsive to his affection, frustrated when he is forgetful, angry at his lack of income? You have a right to all of your feelings and needs, but you owe your partner respect. Your actions and words have the power to enhance his self-worth or to severely harm it. How does your spouse see herself when you fail to call to tell her that you will be late, when you refuse to visit with her family, when you mock her in public or private, when you ignore projects that she has asked you to complete, when you eat or drink more than she thinks wise? Again, you have your own feelings and needs regarding any of these issues—feelings that you need to share responsibly. You deserve to feel at least as attractive, desirable, intelligent, and competent as your partner truly sees you. Your partner deserves the same. You each have the responsibility for providing a true reflection to one another of your unique specialness. As E. E. Cummings urged, "Be of love a little more careful than of everything."

## We Need to Talk to Spur Our Partner's Growth

Being careful in love doesn't imply being silent when your partner's behavior offends you, hurts you, or otherwise concerns you. It means that you care for your partner, and that care demands that you speak honestly. It means also that you are careful in the manner in which you say what you need to say. You need your partner to be all that he or she can be. Therefore, in your central relationship you need to talk clearly and caringly when you perceive your partner is acting in unproductive, immature ways. He or she needs the bracing honesty of your observations. If he talks too loudly or in a self-absorbed manner when you are out with friends, he needs to hear how his behavior affects you. If she acts pushy when she's talking to a salesperson, she needs you to help her to uncover why she behaves this way. If she is starting to drink too much, she might need the help that your words could provide. You need to talk about what bothers you when the behavior occurs, not after so many occurrences have happened that you then explode or withdraw in distance and silence.

You are your partner's greatest source of motivation to grow. You want to develop your talents to be your best self, and you need your partner to assist you in that goal, like a good swimmer or skier needs a good coach. No one sees you as up close and personal as your spouse does. One wife remarked, "One of the nice things about marriage is that you have someone you can ask, 'Do you see this odd thing on my back?' or someone you can talk to about your hemorrhoids and not be afraid that you will hear 'Oh, gross.'" An old mouthwash commercial used to say about bad breath, "Even your best friends won't tell you." Probably no one but your partner will risk telling you about an odd habit you are forming, a verbal tic you have started, or your pattern of talking with food in your mouth. A long-term intimate relationship can provide the setting in which it is safe to hear helpful feedback and thus to mature. The author Mary Caroline Richards writes movingly on this point in her book *Centering*:

It is difficult to stand forth in one's growing, if one is not permitted to live through the stages of one's unripeness, clumsiness, unreadiness, as well as one's grace and aptitude. Love provides a continuous environment for the revelation for one's self, so that one can yield to life without fear and embarrassment. This is why love is in the strictest sense necessary. It must be present in order for life to happen freely. It is the other face of freedom.

Richards describes an intimate environment in which the partners are free to be themselves. This is the atmosphere you and everyone else want in a relationship. You might be confronted but not shamed, challenged but not ridiculed, criticized but not stifled. You can be silly and serious, funny and sad, passionate and passive, confident and vulnerable. You are not locked into a role that offers no allowance for exception. You don't have to be competent or calm *always*. It's all right if you are impatient and irritable periodically. A healthy, growing relationship provides this liberating climate.

To further that relationship, to make it the fertile environment of growth, you have to be free to talk, to express your challenging perceptions as well as your supporting affirmations. In her book, *The New Peoplemaking,* Virginia Satir asserts:

> I want to love you without clutching, appreciate you without judging, join you without invading, invite you without demanding, leave you without guilt, criticize you without blaming, help you without insulting. If I can have the same from you, then we can truly meet and enrich each other.

## Talking Frees Us from
## Limiting Roles Learned in Childhood

What prevents you and your partner from creating such a spirit in your lives? What keeps you from being as free as you desire and need to be? The answer for most of us is fear and bad habits. You and your spouse, like other couples, start your commitment to each other with ideals and promises. You vow, "We won't bicker like other folks do," "We'll talk about everything," "We'll be best friends forever," "We'll make all decisions together." These seemed like reasonable commitments to fulfill. You loved being together. You talked for hours at a time. What has happened? What you probably didn't realize is that, growing up in your families, you and your spouse learned a whole playbook of behaviors that gradually returned as you formed your new family together. The behaviors you developed as a child to survive or to get attention you probably will start exhibiting as an adult. If in your childhood you were subjected to ridicule or indifference when voicing your deepest feelings, you learned, consciously or not, to keep those feelings to yourself or to share them outside of your family. You probably still tend toward that pattern of behavior. If at home you yelled when you were angry, you probably still yell. If in your family you learned to withdraw or act indifferent when you were hurt, you will be inclined to do the same now; if you played peacemaker in times of family tension, you will tend to play the same role in your present family. These habits surface and undermine the best intentions of being open and honest, receptive, empathic, and free.

Todd is an earnest thirty-two-year-old who shared with us his disillusion with his wife:

> Emma is not the woman I married. We had this dream that we would eventually move to Vermont. We planned to build on a small piece of land that I inherited from my grandfather. We would stick with our values of a self-sustaining way of life and raise our kids to enjoy that kind of lifestyle. Then the baby came and Emma turned into this "soccer mom" who arranges play dates religiously, is fanatic about germs, and is scared stiff that our little girl won't get into the right school. She's only in kindergarten, for God's sake!

The fact is that Emma has not changed from the careful, scheduled person she was in her original family. The family in which Emma grew up operated in perpetual chaos. The disorder created in Emma a deep insecurity and an intense embarrassment that her family was the peculiar one of the neighborhood. Emma developed a controlling way of coping with life circumstances. She was terrified of doing anything "unusual" that would cause her friends to regard her as "odd." Now, as a young mother, Emma has reverted to familiar habits. She wants herself and Todd to fit in, to look "right," and their child to be safe and secure.

Emma and Todd need to talk—not judge and counterjudge. Emma has to articulate her fears of being socially rejected or of doing anything that puts their child in jeopardy. She has to convey to Todd how these fears make her reluctant now to move to Vermont where she imagines them as odd-looking outsiders exposing their daughter to all kinds of threats. Todd must voice his disappointment that they are developing a lifestyle antithetical to their original plans. He needs Emma to understand his consternation that she seems to have forgotten their dream of being in the woods in Vermont. Only when they are both willing to share their feelings and brave the other's anger, defensiveness, or disappointment will they be able to come together. Together they can prompt one another's growth. With *accurate* knowledge about one another, they can make realizable plans for the future. But they need to talk.

Richard is a sought-after psychologist who grew up in a household coping with illness. His mother was prone to hysterics and his disabled father was unable to work. Richard's two older brothers left the house for college and kept away even for most vacations. In order to cope with his parents, Richard learned to please. But beneath his good-boy behavior he was deeply resentful of his parents for his lack of freedom to be himself and of his brothers for abandoning him. He came to us for counseling. He described being distant from his wife and very tempted to have an affair with another psychologist in his practice. Despite his training, he was unaware that his childhood resentments were reemerging at home towards his wife. He described trying to please her and of not being free to be himself around her. The only way that he could imagine being happy was to get away, but he felt guilty.

Richard is a sensible and caring man. He has the very qualities that serve him well as a psychologist and that enabled him to play the good-boy role he took on as a child. In therapy he was able to identify the patterns that made him feel trapped and resentful. Yet even with intellectual awareness, he finds that the old habits he had learned in childhood die hard. In order to change, Richard now has to focus each day, and in each interaction with his wife, in order to assert his needs and his preferences. Slowly he is becoming freer and less resentful. For

Richard, the consequences of not talking, of not feeling free to assert himself, were resentment, distance from his wife, and thoughts of infidelity. Like Richard, you need to reflect on attitudes and behaviors that you learned in your original family and that have surfaced in your new one. You, too, will have to work each day to be free of the habits that you developed long ago in order to survive but that are now unnecessary and unhelpful.

## Talking Makes for Good Decision-Making

Couples make a multitude of decisions that affect their lives together. In order to ensure that these decisions unite a couple rather than divide them, both partners need to be involved in decision-making. Whether the decision involves selecting a new house or car, deciding to invest in property, or choosing if, when, and where to take a vacation, both partners need to be free to express their feelings and preferences. The process of deciding can invite both of them to consider their own values and preferences and to discover what matters most to their partner. A couple that arrives at a decision together is more likely to remain committed to it. Together they take ownership for their choice; together they enjoy or suffer its consequences.

Tony and Janice considered getting a new kitchen for their charming but old house. Tony described their collaboration:

> It wasn't pretty, but we got there in the end. Janice was most into doing the renovation. Makes sense, she's a gourmet cook. We looked at numbers and agreed on an amount we could spend. That was surprisingly easy. Then we went to kitchen showrooms and I could see Janice getting excited with the salespeople as if she was going to get the best of everything. It scared the hell out of me. I envisioned the price doubling. She was mad at me because, she said, I was keeping her from having her dream kitchen. I was mad at her because it seemed like she lost her head when we went looking for cabinets and countertops. We stuck to our promise, though, that we would talk throughout the whole process. We had some horrendous arguments, but we finally agreed on a kitchen that was pretty close to budget. We

both can live with the price and the kitchen and, thank God, with each other.

A similar project caused so much tension that it brought a couple into counseling. David and Marissa decided to finish their basement when their twin sons turned thirteen. They didn't have a lot of money left at the end of each month, but they felt confident that they could redo the basement without too much of a financial strain. When their boys asked Marissa if they could have a big screen television and a computer with Internet access, Marissa told them to ask their father. He was appalled that the boys would ask for such expensive "toys" and that Marissa would put him in the position to deny their requests. In his anger he lashed out at Marissa and the twins, calling her a baby and the boys selfish and spoiled. The next day he canceled the entire project.

To understand what happened in this situation, Marissa and David had to examine the way that they interact on all issues. Marissa tends to play the role of the little girl asking David's permission for things she wants or actions she wishes to take. The role doesn't require her to know their finances or to understand David's concerns. In the role she plays, her *modus operandi* is to know what she wants and then to get it by effective but indirect ways. Sometimes she tries to charm and cajole David in flirtatious fashion. At other times she attempts to manipulate by pouting childishly. David plays the authoritarian father-boss role. He takes on all of the responsibility and does all the deciding. He controls the finances and prides himself on the amount of money he provides to run the household.

For the first years of their marriage, the arrangement served both of them. Marissa had a lifestyle she enjoyed. David had the control he desired. But for some time before the basement showdown, each was feeling dissatisfied. David was feeling financial pressure and impatience with Marissa's lack of concern. Marissa was chafing under the restrictions that David imposed on her. They each needed to talk. As they did, they learned about themselves; David came to understand his need to control, and Marissa came to face her avoidance of accountability. They listened to one another and together and individually they started to change.

David and Marissa had slipped into roles that were at first comfortable but in fact kept each spouse from growing. The roles were impediments to genuine connection. Many couples slide into roles in which their deepest needs and feelings are not expressed. These couples need to talk. They have to voice these deep feelings and needs, and they have to listen and understand one another. Such honest, often painful, interactions can uncover roles that they had not admitted to previously, or that they might have thought were justified responses to the other's expectations or behavior.

Jean and Ted were married only two years when Ted was offered a job in Connecticut. He accepted the job and moved east, while Jean stayed in Ohio to complete her master's degree. After a month, Ted called Jean and announced, "I found us a house! You'll love it. I put a down payment on it today and it will be ready for us when you finish in May." Jean was crushed. She remained angry for a year, not only because he had chosen a house without her input, but also that she didn't "love" it. Months later when Jean first came for counseling, she and Ted were close to ending their young marriage.

Jean's response to the situation had been to feel depressed and to complain weakly to Ted. "It's not fair. You should have let me see the house before you bought it. Whatever made you think that you could make that decision?" Jean needed to learn to assert herself decisively and not to whine. In counseling, she realized that she had expected Ted to be the leader, to be as her father had been in her family. But Ted is not the executive her father was and is not blessed with his judgment or confidence. Jean actually demonstrates far better judgment than Ted does in making long-range plans. Ted is impulsive and impractical— flaws that plague his career. Yet Jean had unconsciously thrust Ted into a role that she was more qualified to fulfill. Ted had taken the proffered reins rather than admit his feelings of inadequacy. With the wrong one leading, they had wandered from one bad choice to another. Ted hid his vulnerability behind a rigid, domineering façade. Jean became the defeated victim of his unchallenged mistakes. They had unwittingly formed a dysfunctional relationship in which the wrong one led. Eventually, Jean and Ted learned to realize how they had suffered when they failed to act in unison. Through difficult but revelatory discussions, they decided that Jean should take over the finances. She would lead the way in situations that demanded practical thinking. To make decisions in unison they had to talk openly about their differences. Ted had to admit to his impulsiveness, and Jean had to own her tendency to be passive and then to blame and punish. Thanks to their candid admissions, Ted and Jean have been able to dismantle old and ineffective roles. They realize that they will need heightened awareness to keep from slipping back into old habits. They are committed to continuing to admit their feelings. As Ted said, "If we don't, we'll be back hurting each other, and we've had too much of that." They are more likely now to express their feelings openly than to act out of them in harmful ways.

## You Need to Talk, and So Does Your Partner

In order to break the habits of poor communication that you and your partner have developed, you first have to identify them. Responding to these questions might help you and your partner to focus on your relationship:

- What feelings are you hesitant to express?

- What needs are you reluctant to share?

- What opinions or views do you keep to yourself?

- What topics are off limits?

- What feelings, views, or needs of your partner are threatening to you or are most difficult to hear?

- What would you most like him or her to understand?

- What do you think your partner would most like you to understand?

- In what way does your partner communicate that most annoys you?

- What do you do that most annoys your partner?

When you have clarified the habits that you and your partner practice—habits that don't help you to connect, that lead to frustration and misunderstanding—then you need a plan to change them. Goodwill and good intentions are not enough to make changes effectively. You have to stop behaviors that haven't worked but are now habitual. You need to start demonstrating new behaviors that free you to be honest and lead you to understanding and connection.

## Rituals Can Be Helpful

A couple we counseled complained that they had no time to talk. They each worked, got home around 6:00 p.m., played with their three-year-old, made dinner, put the baby to bed, did the dishes, maybe watched a little television, and then went to sleep. Where, they asked us, did we think they could find time to talk? We answered that, despite the pressing demands, they had to carve out time for one another. Talking together is not a luxury. It is a necessity. We counseled them to put aside one night a week when the babysitter stayed into the evening. That evening they would meet somewhere after work, have dinner, and walk together before going home. They would make a concerted effort to share the feelings that they had been experiencing at work, at home, towards one another, about their child, and about anyone else. Their weekly night now has become sacred to them. They try never to miss it. They tell us they are amazed at the difference it has made in their feelings toward each other.

Establishing a predictable time and place to talk is a way of developing a ritual that guarantees attention to one another. In general, rituals are practices that are established to celebrate a value. The observance of the ritual makes the value more real in the lives of those who participate in it. For instance, the national anthem precedes all major-league baseball games. Singing the anthem celebrates and intensifies the value that Americans have in loving their flag and their country. Fireworks on the Fourth of July commemorate for Americans their independence as a country and allow them a moment to realize their good fortune. Rituals are set; participants know that they are coming. They can look forward to them and prepare for them. They can count on them to fulfill and enrich values they hold dear. Couples valuing intimacy know that closeness can be threatened by the press of work and childrearing and the pull of responsibilities. They need rituals to counterbalance these pressures and foster the intimacy that they value.

A ritual that we recommend to most couples is that they set aside twenty minutes or half an hour to talk to one another in a very defined format every day or at least five days a week. As much as possible they should meet at the same time each day and in the same place (dining room, den, or bedroom). One begins by sharing feelings experienced that day. The other's job is only to listen. Then they change roles. The one who was speaking now listens while the one who was listening now shares a feeling. Often couples resist setting up this ritual for a great variety of reasons, but those who develop the ritual and remain faithful to it describe to us the positive effect this predictable sharing time has on their relationship.

Couples can build other intimacy-creating rituals. A husband and wife we know take a car trip once a month, swearing that the enclosed setting of the car provides a place for a mutually captive audience. They are free from distractions; they turn off their cell phones and are available only to one another. Another couple told us that at the beginning of each year they make an annual "retreat" of three days during which they share their deepest feelings, review the most meaningful events of the past year, and make plans for the year to come. One couple described a park with a small pond where they go whenever they have to talk through an important decision: "Just being there grounds us in the seriousness of our intention to tackle an issue." Rituals can help you to break habitual patterns of poor communication. They force you and your partner to dedicate time to focus on your values. The result of such rituals and focus is intimacy.

## We Need to Be Affirming of Our Partners

Intimacy is fed by affirmation—words and actions that express appreciation, respect, support, love. You are capable of those words and actions and so is your partner. How free are both of you to express them? You need affirmation even if sometimes you might feel embarrassed or unworthy to accept it. And so does your spouse, no matter how awkward his or her response. The danger is that you might allow the awkwardness to discourage you from expressing the affirmation as well as from receiving it.

Think about the last time that you said to your partner:

- I am grateful for all the work that you do for us.

- I respect you
  + for your values.
  + for the way that you treat your parents.
  + for the way you care for your body.
  + for the way you work.

- I admire
  + your ability to be calm.
  + your generosity.
  + your strength.
  + your spontaneity.
  + your ability to laugh at yourself.

- I appreciate
  + your thoughtfulness.
  + your kindness.
  + your promptness.

- I love
  + the way you look.
  + your face.
  + your voice.
  + your sense of humor.
  + the way you walk.

- I love you.

If you are embarrassed to voice these kinds of affirmations to your partner, get over it; or at least don't let your embarrassment deprive your partner from hearing your true feelings. An elderly woman talked to us about her husband of fifty-six years who had died recently after a long ordeal with cancer. "He told me every day how lucky he was to have me. He would say, 'I love you,' like he did when we were kids. Maybe that's why he made me feel young and beautiful." In contrast, a middle-aged woman shared with us, "I'm sure Jim loves me. I tell him that I love him. I stopped for a while but that felt awful. Maybe it's silly, but I'd love to hear him say it to me." Words matter. They are the currency of intimacy. They can reach down into the depth and truth of your feelings and allow those feelings to be visible to the one you love most. Words can help you to realize how much you are feeling towards your spouse. They can reveal you to yourself while they convey your essential core to your partner. Sharing yourself is risky. You might feel foolish and naked and fearful of being misunderstood. It is a risk worth taking. We've never heard anyone regret expressing appreciation and love. We have often heard the awful regret of someone saying, "I wish to God I had told him how I felt."

> **Sharing yourself is risky. You might feel foolish and naked and fearful of being misunderstood.**

Though words are of paramount importance in communicating our appreciation and love, actions can sometimes speak louder. A handsome, athletic sixty-year-old talked to us about his wife of thirty-five years. "She's a very loving woman. She knows me. She knows when I need to get away and doesn't read it as rejecting her. She knows I hate being late and really makes an effort to be on time. A lot of things like that. I try to do the same for her. We're lucky." Some of our clients cherish their partners' signs of affection—hugs, kisses, holding their coats, stroking their hair. Others feel the absence. "She doesn't even get up when I come home from work." "He never touches me except when he wants sex." "We used to hold hands. I envy other couples when I see them walking along together arm-in-arm or holding hands." "I wish she hugged me the way she hugs the kids." "We haven't kissed in years except a peck now and then, not a real kiss." Maybe you and your partner need to talk about the physical affection you desire. Do you know what pleases and what disappoints you both? Ignorance in this situation is not bliss but is cause for hurt and frustration.

## Honesty with Self Leads to Honesty with Others

Honesty with yourself is the basis for trusting yourself and the starting place for being honest with others; being honest with your partner establishes trust between the two of you. When you refuse to admit to yourself your feelings, intentions, views, and prejudices, you cut yourself off from yourself. Such reluctance is usually combined with a refusal to admit to your partner what you really feel and think. You can't give what you haven't got. The feelings you deny to yourself are feelings you can't share with your partner.

We have observed questionable behaviors that proceed from such denial, for example, the roars of a red-faced guy insisting, "I'm not angry." We've challenged the teenage client who is consistently absent or late for classes and complains frequently of headaches. Yet she refuses to admit her feelings of anxiety about not fitting in or having friends, feelings that explain her behavior and physical condition. We've confronted a young man who won't acknowledge his feelings of shame and fear about his drug use, while his denial interferes with his recovery. Feelings and behaviors often conflict with self-image. "I'm not afraid to go on job interviews," proclaims the strong young man, despite much evidence to the contrary. The young girl who dresses provocatively and sees herself as "cool" or "stylish" doesn't want to admit that the way she dresses could be seductive. Businessmen and -women insist that their motives are ethical while they rationalize cheating on their expense accounts or shading the truth from a client.

> Honesty with yourself is the basis for trusting yourself and the starting place for being honest with others.

It is easy to fool oneself while maintaining an image of respectability. But down deep, at some level, the self-deception cannot hold. At some level when people lie to themselves they know it. The result is self-dislike, even self-hatred, and certainly

**Acknowledging your intentions and feelings to yourself is crucial for honesty with your partner.** self-distrust. If your intention in making a remark is to make yourself seem more sophisticated than the person you are with, admit it to yourself, and then reflect on your need to appear superior. If you catch yourself bad-mouthing someone at work, ask yourself what you are feeling towards your coworker and how these feelings are affecting you. Acknowledge feelings of are envy, anger, or sexual attraction—these feelings are not evil. They reveal you to yourself—your insecurities, needs, and drives. Not admitting them can lead to behaviors that are destructive. Admitting them can be sources of insight into yourself as well as warning lights that might suggest caution.

Acknowledging your intentions and feelings to yourself is crucial for honesty with your partner. Shakespeare, as usual, has it right:

> This above all: to thine own self be true,
> And it must follow as the night the day
> Thou canst not then be false to any man.

The great Spanish novelist Miguel de Cervantes urges, "Make it thy business to know thyself, which is the most difficult lesson in the world." Revealing your intentions and feelings to your partner allows you to be known and trusted while encouraging your partner to be open with you. In other words, your transparency can prompt the same from your partner. When you reveal your fears, it is safer for him to reveal his. When he hears your willingness to admit to feelings of self-doubt or inferiority, he can feel less vulnerable in voicing similar feelings. Your acknowledgment of needs for privacy or pleasure makes his more acceptable. Each of you can experience the relief that transparency often provides as well as the trust it engenders.

Trust in itself fosters self-revelation. When you trust your spouse, you are drawn to open yourself to him—your experiences, thoughts, and feelings. You hope that his trust in you invites similar openness. Trust opens the way to give your selves to one another. Distrust has the opposite effect. When you distrust, you pull back and are guarded, evasive, even secretive. Trust allows for transparency and nourishes intimacy.

## Body Language Also Communicates

When you are disgusted, your body expresses your emotion: you shake your head or you groan. Other emotions prompt you to roll your eyes, tap your fingers, raise your eyebrows, look away, or laugh out loud. You reveal the truth of what you feel in a whole variety of bodily expressions. These behaviors, like your words, can inform you about yourself. If you are tapping your feet, checking your watch, and rubbing your eyes, what feelings are you demonstrating? Your body is telling you about you, and you need to listen to it. It is also communicating to your partner. Be alert to the message that you are sending or that she is receiving. Are the sent messages and the received messages congruent?

A couple in marriage counseling exchanged verbal blows about non-verbal slights. Shawna angrily said, "I think he's passive aggressive. I read about it in a magazine and I thought, 'This is my husband.'" Her husband looked shocked and said, "What on earth are you talking about?" "Oh, you know what I mean," Shawna countered. "Whenever I drive the car, you put your seat belt on as if you are preparing for battle. You grab the dashboard when I head for an on-ramp to the highway. If I pass a car you hold your breath. You do the same kind of thing when we are out with our friends. If I make a joke you put your head back and roll your eyes as if I'm an idiot." Her husband was quick to charge, "Shawna, you're no saint. What was going on with you when I tried to hold your hand at your job and you pulled it away as if I had attacked you?"

Body language that conveys a critical or dismissive message is often unfair and somewhat cowardly. Since no words have been spoken, the message is difficult for the recipient to dispute and easy for the sender to deny. Yet your body does express you. Gestures can help you to emphasize your impatience or communicate your care. Some people would be greatly handicapped if they couldn't use their hands while talking. But trust is threatened when body language, instead of enhancing verbal communication, is careless and irresponsible. Your body's language can be a genuine part of your self-expression. It can help you to convey the fullness of your message and it can reveal to yourself feelings and attitudes of which you were unaware. It can be a wonderful shorthand and provide a code between partners who really know one another. We have heard remarks such as, "I know when he gets that look that he is ready to pack it in and go home," "She starts tapping her foot when she doesn't like where the conversation is heading," "Her body begins to droop, but she doesn't realize she's tired," "When he leans forward a certain way I know he's going to start dominating and lecturing." Couples communicate to one another through their bodies, and sometimes no words need to be said.

Your relationship with your partner is central to the way you view yourself. It can be incredibly life-giving, growth-prompting, and joy-producing. At the same time it has the potential to sap life and breed feelings of hopelessness and despair. Probably in no other relationship is talking openly and honestly more essential. You need to talk with your partner and you need to learn how to talk in a way that creates trust, fosters intimacy, stimulates mutual growth, and provides the profound satisfaction of being truly known and loved.

■   F O R   R E F L E C T I O N   ■

1.  Does your partner motivate you to grow? What does he or she say that prompts this growth?

2.  What have you shared with a partner that prompted him or her to take stock and to grow?

3.  Are there roles that you play in this central relationship that prevent you from being free to speak openly?

4. Can you recall a time when you and your partner, through discussion, arrived at a very satisfying decision?

5. Have you and your partner developed rituals that guarantee time to talk—every day, every week?

# Chapter Three

# *talking between parents and children*

> The real art of conversation is not only to say the right thing at the right time, but also to leave unsaid the wrong thing at the tempting moment.
>
> —Lady Dorothy Nevill

## We Need to Talk to Create Talk-Friendly Environments in Our Families

We need to talk in our family; after all, that is the place where we learn to talk. We learn that we can talk freely and openly and that what we say is heard and respected, or we learn to be quiet to avoid indifference, criticism, or ridicule. Our family is our first and most important place of learning. We learn to speak as our parents speak (or don't speak). If they are bilingual, we learn to speak in two languages. If they are comfortable with the language of emotions and reason, we learn to express our feelings as well as our reasoned thoughts. Parents set the tone and provide the example for the way that the family communicates. Children are like sponges, absorbing the family's way of talking. One couple described their differences in style of communicating by referring back to their original families. The vivacious woman said, "We were a family of screamers so I scream. I wish I didn't, but I do. His family is *sooo* quiet. It's unbelievable. So he doesn't like it when I yell, but that's better than not talking, isn't it? I don't know what he's thinking."

Wise parents realize that creating a loving environment in which every family member's contribution is respected begins with them. Their example of respect for one another is a model for their children to follow. Their approach to talking to each other and to each child and the respectful way in which they listen guide the children to similar behavior. Parents create the family's style of interaction, but not merely by example. Consciously they create rituals in which mutually respectful expression is encouraged. Family meetings and sit-down dinners create opportunities that prompt talking together. For example, the late Joe Kennedy, patriarch of the famous Kennedy family, used family dinners to encourage informed discussions. He would introduce a topic of national or international significance and expect reflective, reasoned responses from all of the children. Some parents organize family outings, car trips, or breakfasts after church or temple services to bring the family together in a way that promotes interaction.

One family that we met recently demonstrated the effect of parents' emphasis on the importance of active communication in their family. After twenty years of military duty, Wilson, the father, a colonel in the air force, was retiring from military service. He and his wife, Tina, and their four children were embarking on a new phase of their lives with a slate of choices to make. To begin with, they had to decide where to live: in the United States or in one of the countries where they had been stationed and had come to love? They wanted to take a fresh look at both Wilson's and Tina's careers. Would she return to the nursing profession and would he go back to school? Their twins were

> Parents set the tone and provide the example for the way that the family communicates.

about to enter high school. How did the next four years of their education figure into the formula for settling on a location? An entirely different option was always in their thoughts: was it possible to work as a family for the next couple of years at a mission in Africa where the parents had once volunteered? With so many questions and variables, the family felt nearly paralyzed. Wilson and Tina made a critical decision. They recognized that the conclusions they would come to would affect everyone in the family. The future of each person's life would be shaped by the choices that they would make today. Clearly, they reasoned, each person—even the smallest, the eight-year-old—had a right to have a say. They resolved to make these decisions as a family. Over several months the parents and the children had weekly discussions that they came to call their "family board meetings." During these meetings every person was given time to talk about their hopes, dreams, and fears. Each had assignments to research and to present when they came together.

Wilson and Tina created an environment and even a structure that invited and valued the contribution of all of the children. In this environment each person was expected to offer his or her feelings, thoughts, needs, preferences, and opinions. Assignments of specific areas of research and reflection encouraged responsible contribution. The family considered the consequences of possible decisions, and, eventually, they worked out a plan. Through their "board meetings" they learned a lot about each other. They realized that they were reluctant to stop traveling and that they wanted to do something meaningful as a family. But they also acknowledged their need to put down roots. One of their sons wanted to attend a military high school while his twin wanted to go to public school. Finally, Wilson and Tina's family resolved to stay in the United States not too far from a high school military academy. Their summers and vacations would be committed to working for Habitat for Humanity.

Wilson and Tina valued family discussion and through it taught their children to speak up, to speak responsibly, and to appreciate the views of others. Not all decisions, of course, can or should be made by family consensus. Whether a three-year-old can play alone near a busy street or whether a teenager can drive without a permit are not up for discussion. Parents have to use good judgment to recognize when to discuss and when to decide.

Encouraging your children to talk, however, should not mean a license for unfettered self-expression. Children have to be taught to be sensitive to the feelings of others, and to listen to and respect views that might be contrary to theirs. They have to learn when to be quiet as well as when to speak. Parents need to avoid extremes between enforcing a stifling message that children should be "seen and not heard" and fostering an equally unproductive one that permits unbridled, undisciplined venting without any consideration for others. Finding that balance and implementing it in a myriad of settings and situations is the task of every parent. It comes with practice.

## Parents Need to Talk to Guide and Teach

Children have to be taught; parents have to teach. There is no avoiding the fact that children, as we indicated earlier, are sponges soaking up knowledge from their parents. Children see and hear their mothers gossiping, their fathers complaining, and their parents making bigoted or racist remarks. They absorb and they imitate. They hear each parent speak in an informed way about politics and world affairs and they learn. They watch parents be generous to the less fortunate and friendly to neighbors, and their own behaviors are shaped by these observations. Children will learn from each parent—Mom's gentleness with animals and love of hiking, Dad's love of music and joy in camping. But as much as children acquire knowledge from example, they also need to be taught in clear, spoken language, delivered at the appropriate moment, the values, beliefs, and customs that their parents espouse.

We have witnessed parents voicing their values at the right moment: "We don't ever laugh at the disabled," says a mother to a child imitating a classmate's stutter. "Don't throw the soda can in the water. We have to take care of the earth, not make it ugly," responds a dad to a little boy who had thrown an empty soda can into a stream. "You have to put a third of what you earn into your savings account. It's important to save for things you'll want to buy in the future," declares a dad to his sixteen-year-old on the first day of her new job. "Make sure you rehearse the Passover questions that you will be asking tonight," a mother reminds her daughter before the Seder. Children need to hear you articulate what you cherish and value in order to learn about you and their heritage.

As parents you need to talk to each other to clarify the values that you want to convey to your children as well as how and when to do so.

**As parents you need to talk to each other to clarify the values that you want to convey to your children as well as how and when to do so.**

Clarifying conversations can shine light on your own values as well as enable the deeper understanding of those of your partner. You might start by each partner listing values that are a personal priority. Prioritizing your values requires that you reflect together on what you stand for and what you wish to impart to your children. One couple wrote down their list of values:

| Husband | Wife |
|---|---|
| Be honest. | Be generous. |
| Stick to a commitment. | Be loyal to family and friends. |
| Work hard. | Be responsible. |
| Be grateful. | Be prayerful. |
| Be kind. | Be honest. |
| Love God. | Be obedient. |

They weren't surprised at what the other had written and readily agreed with the other's values. They were particularly pleased, however, to see and hear so clearly that they were in harmony.

Parents who are united are effective teachers. Divided they fail, and the children suffer. Divided they undermine one another's authority, and the children lose clear direction. One mother griped, "We agreed that the kids would have definite bedtimes on school nights, but the minute they want to stay up late to watch a television show their father immediately says it's okay. How can we teach them to abide by the bedtime if he lets them change the time so easily?" Similarly, a father objects when his wife goes to the crying baby who has been put to bed for the night. "We discussed how we were going to handle him when he cries; we made a plan, and then she did the opposite."

It is tempting to accuse your partner of being inconsistent in the enforcement of a value-oriented plan and to do so in front of the children. But the blame erodes your partner's credibility and ultimately the effectiveness of both of you. If you are disappointed or frustrated with your partner's parenting, speak up but do so away from the kids. Discuss the incident that concerned you and try to discover what led you or your partner to abandon the previous plan. Sensible discussion can identify the feelings or needs that make it difficult for either of you to be consistent. You might be reacting to one another; for example, if one of you judges the other as being too harsh, then he or she might try to compensate by being lenient. But children prosper when you are consistent and united. Mutually respectful conversations are essential to establishing and maintaining that unity. Promoting values to your children with consistent effort will require ongoing conversations between the two of you. The interactions can keep you both honest and help you to resist temptations to abandon agreed-upon plans of action. They can benefit both you and your children.

Divorced parents can sometimes find it particularly difficult to agree on values of child-rearing. Unless divorced parents are especially mindful, they can thwart one another's plans for the child. Their adversarial behavior is often driven by a conscious or unconscious desire to hurt the ex-spouse, but just as often it hurts the child. A mother complained to us about her ex-husband's parenting of their four-year-old:

> When she comes back from being with him I feel like I have to start all over. I've told him she can't drink caffeinated sodas and she tells me that she had Coke. She hasn't had a nap so when she comes home she's cranky and I have to deal

with the tantrums. It's one thing after another like that. I know it's to get back at me.

Ideally, the couple should meet, possibly with a counselor, to try to establish values that they can agree to impart and rules that they agree to enforce. If these efforts are not possible, then a parent can communicate simply to the child that what is permissible in one house may not be allowed in the other. Though divorced parents may not always agree on expectations regarding daily routines, often they will be able to unite over more significant, shared values that they hope to convey to their children.

Parents who communicate with respect for one another continue to discover their values as they respond to incidents regarding their children. One family encountered just such an opportunity to clarify values. Ira is a young boy at boarding school who described to his parents how he dealt with a friend who "borrowed" his homework and handed it in to the teacher as his own. The next time the friend asked to see Ira's homework, Ira told him, "I heard the teacher say that your paper looked suspiciously like mine. He said that anyone who cheats gets an automatic failure." He hadn't heard the teacher say this, but he thought he could discourage his friend from using his work by scaring him into thinking that he could get into trouble. When he told his parents, his mother praised him for his ingenious way of getting out of a sticky situation. His father was disturbed by his lie.

By talking honestly to each other, Ira's parents were able to realize that they each held a value that the other respected— creative thinking and truthfulness. Then they were able to guide Ira, united in their values but maintaining different perspectives. Mom showed her respect for and delight with Ira's resourceful approach to his problem. Dad discussed with Ira his concern that Ira not become comfortable with lying as a means to avoid confronting difficult circumstances. Mom did not undermine their shared concern for honesty; Dad did not disparage imaginative thinking. Ira was affirmed and guided. Mom, Dad, and Ira learned about themselves and about one another. This process of discovery is not a one-time conversation; it is a dynamic that has to persist throughout their relationship.

Not all parents can demonstrate the self-awareness of Ira's parents, but they do have a responsibility to know their own values and to respect one another's. They also are obliged to examine their motivations when speaking. Lack of awareness of these intentions leads to ambiguous lessons. A mother who hounds her child to write a thank-you note to Grandma for her gift, motivated not by the value of gratitude and consideration but by fear of what her mother-in-law would think of her, teaches a value that doesn't ring true to the child. The father who berates his son for quitting Scouts, not because he values commitment to a pledge but because Scouts had meant so much in his own childhood, tends to leave his son resentful and confused. These parents are pursuing a double agenda. The lessons of gratitude and commitment are being taught, but the parents' self-serving second agenda tends to undermine the lessons. Trust suffers when real intentions are masked. Better to tell Missy that you fear Nana's opinion or tell Johnny that you are disappointed because of what Scouts meant to you. Children probably surmise the truth on some level and will trust you more for admitting it.

## Parents Need to Talk to Communicate Expectations

A frustrated mother was complaining to us about her teenager. "I'm so fed up with her. Every Sunday she stays in bed. She doesn't go to church with us. She's out late Saturday night and then sleeps all morning on Sunday." When we asked her what she had said to her daughter about her expectations, she replied irritably, "For heaven's sake, she should know better. My husband and I always go to church on Sunday. He sings in the choir. We never thought we would have to tell her." The mother admitted that neither she nor her husband had actually made their expectations clear, not only about their daughter's attendance at church but even about her curfew for Saturday nights. She acknowledged gradually that they both feared conflict with their daughter and avoided expressing their preferences on any topic that could lead to conflict. As a result the girl had to guess at her parents' expectations. She might assume that her parents would like her to be home earlier or to attend church services, but since they had never said anything she chose to please herself and to ignore their irritability. Children do not automatically know their parents' expectations. Children need to hear them stated clearly, and they need to realize that their parents are serious when they voice their expectations. They have to hear not only what the expectation is but that their parents definitely anticipate compliance. A father described to us his progress in enforcing his expectations.

Children want to know what parents expect from them. They want order and they want consistency.

> I made it very clear that there would be no television or computer games on school nights. They had far too many school activities and too much homework to allow for distractions. At first they moaned and sulked, but more and more now it's just a given. Actually, I had a harder time than they did giving up TV during the week.

This father is living a value of his own: "Be true to what you believe." He is willing to endure the price of his children's resistance and in doing so provides them with what they really need: consistent direction.

Children want to know what parents expect from them. They want order and they want consistency. From an early age, children push at their boundaries, but they are more secure and peaceful when they know exactly what is required of them. So as a parent, be sure you state clearly and calmly what you expect and the reason for your expectation. Beware of engaging in fruitless, escalating debates with your children. Responsible attention to their views is quite different from endless explanations to their objections. An alert and wise parent knows when to listen and when to put a stop to resistance. Know what you want, make it clear, and make it happen. That's your job.

## Parents Need to Talk to Affirm and Support

Children have to be loved unconditionally. But they also have to *hear* that they are liked, admired, respected, and delighted in for themselves and for very specific behaviors. Parents have enormous power that children can grumble about: power to say no to a sleepover, a new computer, or pair of jeans. But their deeper power is to provide the support and affirmation that gives the child self-worth and confidence, self-esteem and happiness. Children are prone to self-dislike, a universal condition that we have labeled "psychological original sin." The parent has the power to shield and even relieve the child of this tendency by heartfelt affirmation. As a parent, don't assume that your children know that you admire them. Tell them. Even if they trust that you admire them, it is another thing altogether to hear it from you. Be specific. Let them hear what you feel towards them for a particular behavior. Connect your feelings to your child's action. "I'm grateful that you took care of your sister this morning." "I respect the way you brought your grade up from a C." "I love the way you are loyal to your friends and never talk badly about them." "I am so impressed by the poem you wrote." Certainly your children want to hear over and over that you love them. They also crave to hear you voice that love in ways they haven't heard before. You have more impact on them when your words express your present experience in a way unique to this particular moment. Your words find a "fresh place on the pillow" to delight and support your child. A bumper sticker used to ask, "Have you hugged your child today?" We may need a similar reminder, "Tell your child 'I love you' in a new way today."

## We Need to Talk to Set Boundaries

Parents abuse their power at great cost to their children. Even as adults, sons and daughters can be severely impacted by parents' negative, controlling, and critical words. Anthony, a stocky, good-hearted twenty-eight-year-old, came to us for therapy. He was suffering from depression as well as an explosive temper. He worked for his sixty-five-year-old mother in the construction company that his deceased father had founded. Anthony felt controlled by her at work and at home. He felt that he needed to move out of his mother's home to live a free adult life. When he told her of his decision she railed, "You can't leave me. I can't live alone. Besides, you'll never make it on your own." Anthony reported that in the past she had demonstrated the same behavior when he had tried to move out. He knew that this time he had to ignore her words and be firm in asserting himself. "I love you, Mom. I'll never abandon you. But I'm moving out at the end of the month. I'll come for dinner once a week, but I need to get on with my life." Anthony has moved on and moved through his depression and rage, even though his mother has not made it easy.

Eileen is a talented, divorced thirty-two-year-old mother of eight-year-old Andy. After her divorce she moved in with her mother. She came to therapy complaining of anxiety attacks. Though her parents in many ways have been generously supportive, her mother has words to say every day about Eileen's way of raising Andy. "You're spoiling him." "You need to be stricter." "You will reap what you sow with him—there will be problems." "Why do you give him sugar?" Eileen was swallowing her feelings of resentment, anger, and hurt. She was also "self-medicating" with a spending habit that kept her in debt and that consequently required her to continue to live "trapped" with her mother. The suppressed feelings resulted in anxiety attacks.

Eileen needed to talk—to us but also to her mother. Through counseling, she has learned to risk putting her feelings into words.

> I've been firmer with her than I've ever been. Up to now I was always afraid of hurting her feelings. Finally, I told her, "Mom, you've got to stop. You raised me your way. I have to raise Andy my way. I'm too vulnerable to your criticism. I'd rather hear what you think I'm doing right, not what you think I'm doing wrong." We've had big arguments, but we've also had great talks. I'm feeling a great weight off me. Andy and I need a home of our own, but, at least for now, things are much better.

Anthony and Eileen are examples of adult children needing to construct a boundary to a parent's critical words. Yet with some frequency we see in our office elderly parents who have to place a similar kind of boundary on their adult child. Sometimes the adult son or daughter becomes too bossy and controlling towards an aging parent. A well-educated widow described her fear of a son whose phone calls had become more and more stern, "I'm scared to death when he calls. I know he's concerned about me, but he demands an accounting of what I have accomplished in sorting Dad's papers and is furious if I haven't done enough. He's becoming a bully." With some coaching, this woman was able to tell her son that she needed him to speak to her with more gentleness, that she was hurt by his tone, and that she expected him to trust her to do what was necessary. She told us, "I think what I said to him was good for both of us." A similar example of an elderly parent needing to speak up came from Timothy, an elegantly dressed, articulate octogenarian. He described an incident while walking with his son Charles towards a restaurant in Central Park. "Charles is a very impatient man. Twice on the way to the restaurant he barked, 'Come on, let's go. Pick up your feet. We'll miss our reservation.' That's typical of the way he treats me and others. I stopped and told him, 'If you are worried that we'll be late, go ahead. I will not be spoken to in that tone.'"

We counsel parents who need to set a boundary against their adult child's anger. Juan and Angela decided they needed counseling after their daughter Anna refused to allow them to see their two grandchildren. They described her escalating rage at them and their fruitless efforts to resolve her anger. Angela described her last interaction with her daughter.

> We used to talk by phone every day, but then she seemed to be furious with me all the time. She started blaming me for the way I raised her and her brother. Nothing I said seemed to please her. The last time we talked she was so angry that I asked her to come with us to talk to you. She told me to go f— myself and hung up. We haven't heard from her since.

Sometimes constructive dialogue in which grown offspring voice difficult emotions to the parent is necessary. But the parents that we are depicting need to protect themselves from adult children who for varying reasons choose to treat their parents harshly. It might be that the parent seems to be a safe person on which to place blame for their unhappiness or failure. But parents do their son or daughter no good in allowing unproductive tirades. If a parent has demonstrated a concerted and sincere effort to listen and has achieved no resolution, then at some point he or she has to stop talking, stop explaining and defending, and stop allowing verbal onslaughts. Efforts to interact are constructive when two parties genuinely desire to connect with mutual honesty and mutual understanding. When, over time, one party displays a desire only to hurt or to blame, then interacting becomes sadistic for the one trying to hurt and masochistic for the recipient. The one being abused has to say, "No. Enough."

## Examples of Devoted Parents
## Who Encourage Their Children to Talk

In the work we do as psychologists for individuals, couples, and families, we encounter almost every day inspiring examples of parents who create loving environments in which their children can express themselves and blossom. Ironically, though their love is truly admirable, these parents often tend more to self-criticism than to self-congratulation. Bridget is one such parent. She is a recently divorced mother in her thirties who brought her seven-year-old daughter to us "just to make sure that she isn't suffering things from the divorce that I'm not seeing." The little girl, Dariel, chatted away about school, her friends, her dad and mom. Before she left, she asked, "Do you want me to sing for you?" The image of Dariel singing "Mama Mia!" complete with dance moves is a charming picture that stays with us. Her mother thoroughly delights in Dariel and tells her so. It was not surprising then that Dariel was totally confident that *we* would delight in her. She basks in the image of herself that she sees in the mirror of her mother. Dariel's freedom to express herself is a direct reflection of her mother's attentive love. Bridget deserves to acknowledge that she is such a loving mother.

Kelly, a self-described type-A woman in her early forties, is a classic example of a dedicated, loving mother who fails to see her own goodness. She cried hard in her first counseling session. "I'm yelling at the kids. I'm being mean. I'm just like my mother, who was a terrible mother. She left my brothers and me when we were toddlers." During the session we asked Kelly to describe her three daughters. She described each of her children in tender, loving language. She highlighted the unique qualities of each of them and, seemingly without awareness, described the caring way in which she related with each girl. Every week she spends hours with each daughter individually, attentive to each daughter's unique needs and interests. Kelly described how she invites her daughters to share with her their experiences and their concerns:

> Each week I do something special with one of them, like go out for lunch or go shopping or take a walk. I want them to know me, what I have been excited about, what I've been into, and I want to know what is happening with them, what's been bothering them, what they're thinking about. Sometimes I have to prompt them, "Come on, I really want to know." Most of the time they have a ton to say.

Kelly had mentioned that her mother never told her she loved her and never hugged her. When we asked Kelly if she hugged her children and told them she loved them, she said, "Oh, yes." Kelly has to learn to talk to the children firmly without yelling, but she also has to stop condemning herself and realize how the children were truly graced by her devoted love.

Ben is the father of four children under seven years of age. He readily admits to his faults but is able to take pride in being a good dad. He is in his early thirties and refers to his wife, Lara, as his best friend. Ben is dynamic, charismatic, and very successful. He is also a thoroughly attentive father.

> When I'm with my kids, I'm finally peaceful. I love biking and skiing with my son and playing with the younger ones. They're all different. My son's like my little buddy. The girls are great. Guys ask me to play golf on weekends. I couldn't. That is my time with them and with Lara.

Ben described his delight in playing with his children and went on to depict his bedtime rituals with each of them:

> I divide my time with each of the three older ones; the baby I kiss goodnight. I tell them, "OK, I'll tell you something about my day. Then you tell me something. What was good? What wasn't so good?" They amaze me with what they're thinking. I would never know what was going on in their heads if I didn't have these talks with them.

Jon and Indra, married for thirty years, exemplify parental love that remains constant throughout a child's teenage and young-adult crises. Their son Reed, now twenty-six, has struggled with alcoholism since he was a teenager. They described his ordeal and their own as the necessary stimulus towards better communication:

> When Reed started having problems, we had huge arguments. I thought Jon was burying his head in the sand, and he thought I was getting hysterical about ordinary high school stuff. He called Reed's drinking a typical kid phase. But it got worse, and we had to stop arguing and start talking if we were going to help him.

They took to heart the advice the first alcoholism counselor gave to them: "If you want to help your son, you're also going to have to grow and change." They have been steadfast in supporting their son and in confronting their own troubles. The two times that he was admitted to rehabilitation centers, they willingly participated in week-long family therapy programs at the centers. They are proud to say that Reed has been sober for four years. He says he couldn't imagine sobriety without his parents' support and the hours of talking they did in groups and alone as a family.

Parents who neglect and even abuse their children are failures to their sacred trust. Our experience, however, is that many, many parents are utterly devoted to their children. Of course, there is always room for them to learn how to talk to their children more productively, more personally, and with more consistent discipline; but they also deserve to credit themselves for all of their dedication and commitment. Being a parent is an awesome

Talking conscientiously, truthfully, and lovingly is the key to and the measure of a family's health.

responsibility and one that can easily induce feelings of inadequacy or failure. As you learn to relate with your children more effectively, start by being gentler with yourself.

The nature of family is evolutionary. As children mature and parents age, new roles emerge, stresses ebb and flow, crises erupt, and new members are added to the family through marriage or lost through death. To manage well this ever-changing character of families, talking is essential. You can develop a family ethic that encourages talking or one that squelches it. You can foster responsible talking that respects the rights, opinions, and feelings of all the members in the family, or you can allow and even enable one or more members to tyrannize and dominate. As a parent, you create the family environment. It is your challenge to teach your children their responsibility to enhance it. Your home can be a loving, growth-stimulating environment, or it can be filled with tension and fear that cripple development. Talking conscientiously, truthfully, and lovingly is the key to and the measure of a family's health.

## ■ FOR REFLECTION ■

1. *In your home, have you consciously tried to produce an environment that invites everyone to talk?*

2. *Are there times when you are uncomfortable talking with your children? Do you actually talk to them about your discomfort?*

3. *When was the last time you discussed a value with one of your children?*

4. *Can you put into words your expectations about the way your children behave toward you?*

5. *Do you consciously affirm your children? Have you affirmed your spouse in the presence of your children?*

6.  *How do you communicate boundaries to your children? Have you ever found yourself assuming that your children know boundaries that you haven't articulated?*

# Chapter Four

## *talking at work*

If you want to go quickly, go alone.

If you want to go far, go together.

—African proverb

Haynes Johnson and Dan Balz in their book, *The Battle for America 2008*, contrast the candid style of Barack Obama's campaign manager, David Axelrod, with the flattering approach of Hillary Clinton's campaign strategist, Mark Penn. Axelrod warned Obama, "You care far too much what is written and what is said about you. You don't relish combat when it becomes personal and nasty." Meanwhile in Clinton's camp, several of her advisors wanted to refute the image that some voters had of her as cold and distant, but Mark Penn played down this concern and stroked Clinton's ego in a memo to her, saying, "People don't just like Hillary Clinton, they love her." Barack Obama benefited significantly, the authors write, from Axelrod's bracing words. Hillary Clinton, they note, was woefully misled by Penn's flattery. Clinton's strategist did not serve her well. He dismissed critical observations of advisors and instead proffered ones intended to please rather than to inform. Words in the workplace can be idle or self-serving. They can be designed to manipulate or to deceive—a waste of time and worse. Conversely, they can be clarion calls of insight and indicators of integrity and wit.

We need to talk clearly, honestly, and effectively in our work environments. The goal of authentic interaction in families and between friends and partners is intimacy. In workplace settings, the aim of authentic communication, while not intimacy, is still to facilitate trusting relationships. Without trust, an employee will not speak up to his boss, a private to his sergeant, or a student to her teacher. If a doctor does not trust his patient, he will treat her defensively. When a manager fails to trust, she will not delegate assignments. In order for interactions to proceed harmoniously between peers as well as from the top down and from the bottom up, communication that fosters trust is essential.

Honest interaction between employer and employee allows a business to profit from the input of all of its employees. An atmosphere facilitating free expression encourages workers to be themselves, their most creative selves, without fear of repression. Teamwork that is characterized by effective communication harnesses the energy of all of the members toward the company's goals. In the military, when the commander issues unequivocal directions, the troops can respond in a unified manner, free from second-guessing and dissension. When the commander instills trust by his or her unmistakable expression of support, military personnel are free to obey, not as robots but as adults who are able to use their own judgment. Professionals in education, healthcare, and law, for example, are effective to the degree that they have conveyed their commitment to the best interests of their students, patients, and clients. Leaders have to demonstrate their desire to understand as well as their need to be understood.

> In workplace settings, the aim of authentic communication, while not intimacy, is still to facilitate trusting relationships.

Effective communication is the fuel that drives the engine of all productive group effort and the food that nourishes professional care. With it, work environments, classrooms, and offices are satisfying, stimulating places. Without such trusting interaction, they become dysfunctional settings in which people are stymied, sometimes even paralyzed, by discord. Rather than inviting an individual's full potential, toxic work settings crush it. So, since healthy communication is evidently desirable and even essential in the workplace, what gets in its way?

## We Need to Talk to Overcome Fear

Nothing obstructs free expression more than fear. Students won't ask a question if they are afraid of a teacher's sarcasm or ridicule. People looking for financial guidance can be intimidated by the financial advisor's use of jargon. Fear prevents patients from admitting their behaviors and even their symptoms. Jack, for example, minimizes the facts of his cigarette smoking when speaking to his doctor. Jill doesn't admit to her physician how much she eats. Their daughter Jackie lies to her dentist, saying that she flosses daily. Each of them, afraid of the provider's reprimands, impedes the value of the professional appointment. When we were doing research for our book, *Sick and Tired of Feeling Sick and Tired*, we observed that physicians complained about patients refusing to provide information pertinent for effective treatment, while patients described their fear of the physician's judgmental reactions.

Fifty-two-year-old Maureen, who suffers with lupus, confessed to us that she became ill from a medication prescribed by her rheumatologist, yet continued to take it, fearing his disapproval. "He's so sure he is right about this medication, and he gets impatient quickly if I don't agree. I just feel too vulnerable to argue." A real estate agent told us that she had stopped going to her counselor. "I was afraid that she was disgusted with me for staying in an abusive relationship. I'm working up courage to go back to her. She's very good, but tough."

> Fear in the workplace stifles truthful self-expression.

Fear in the workplace stifles truthful self-expression. Carrie shared with her friend that her boss was four months late doing her annual review. Her friend asked, "Why don't you just go in and ask him to do it?" Carrie replied, "I can't. I'm afraid he'll think I'm criticizing him and the way he does his job. Then he might take it out on me and give me a negative review." Ted, Rick, and Emily, experienced salespeople, described with chagrin the situation they have been enduring on the job. Their new managing director proposed an "innovative" way to organize sales data. Three years earlier they had witnessed the same kind of plan fail miserably and were confident this plan would meet a similar end. But a fear of speaking up kept them silent. Now, six months into implementing their manager's data-organizing system, they are watching a doomed project drain resources in company time and money. Fear hampers honesty and hurts business. Pleasing the boss substitutes poorly for genuine service.

In the military, sometimes failure to speak up due to fear is dangerous. An army officer related a life-threatening incident. A master sergeant had ordered an explosive ordnance team to destroy a huge pile of mixed ammunition. The leader of the team realized that there were an insufficient number of Composition C-4 explosives to do the job properly, but fearing the irascible master sergeant, he proceeded with the demolition. Hundreds of these projectiles then blew all over the range and beyond. The master sergeant, acting against safety policies for this type of situation, ordered his detachment to "go pick them up and pile them in one place." Ammunition that receives the improper amount of force will arm itself and become dangerous to pick up by hand. Two leaders of the group advised the men against this action, but no one confronted the master sergeant. The disposal team was now filled with confusion and fear. The threat hanging over them was, "Do it, or lose rank or pay." The alternative threat was death or serious injury.

> The healthier the environment, the less fear controls the behavior of the people in it.

Obedience is vital for military procedure. Insubordination cannot be tolerated. Yet failure to speak up for fear of a superior's wrath can lead to a life-threatening situation. Freedom to speak the truth is important for the individual boss or employee, commander or private, professional or client. The company, hospital, school, or store needs honest individual expression to fulfill its function. But reticence, prevarication, and even out-and-out lying trump the ideal of honesty when fear prevails. The healthier the environment, the less fear controls the behavior of the people in it.

## We Need to Talk to Relay Bad News

Providing good news is a joy. Bosses, doctors, mechanics, or teachers conveying favorable news watch the listener respond with delight, excitement, and relief, and may receive thanks, a hug, or a handshake in return. The same persons who welcome the opportunity to provide an upbeat message dread the duty of delivering bad news. They loathe witnessing disappointment and sadness as much as they fear resentment and anger as the messengers of bad tidings. The prospect of facing sad or irate reactions tempts some in authority to avoid responsibility. Some physician assistants are left to describe to patients the disturbing side effects of a medication because the physician is reluctant to deliver the information. Middle managers are burdened with the responsibility of terminating employees, because the senior managers don't want to face the ex-employees. Few in authority would claim to be skilled at communicating unwelcome news.

John, an Army chief of staff, adheres to the corps' procedure for presenting information: "Be accurate, be brief, and be clear." As a rule he has these skills honed, but he told us that he blunders from being blunt to being defensive when announcing redeployment to troops who yearn to be home. A mortgage broker groaned at the thought of speaking to his clients:

> I was stunned when I heard from a supervisor in the home office that the last three mortgages I had negotiated had been denied. I felt sick. I can only imagine how defeated these potential homeowners will feel. I can't be too apologetic or blame my own bank when I tell them. But I feel for my customers and their dashed hopes. I have to fight putting off the phone call.

On the other hand, some people offend due to naïveté or insensitivity when they fail to comprehend that the information they are delivering could be distressing. Sue, a veteran first-grade teacher, felt confident telling the mother of a six-year-old,

> I think Allen will be a much happier and successful student
> if he repeats first grade. He's the youngest in his class and he
> never really caught up to his classmates. If he goes to second
> grade, he'll always be behind. This way, by repeating first
> grade, he'll be a leader.

Sue wasn't prepared for the mother's utter dismay. Allen's mother dissolved into tears and cried, "Allen will be heartbroken and his father will be furious." Sue learned what many who have to present discouraging news discover—the person to whom you are speaking is not the only one affected. Sue entered the world of the mother, who now has the burden of bringing the news to her child and to her spouse.

Some people who have the responsibility of imparting to others disheartening or frightening information are so awkward that they confuse the facts and fail to address emotions at all. A young woman, Sateesha, who has been suffering with pain for several years, described a recent interaction with her doctor. At the end of the appointment, the doctor wrote out a prescription for a pain reliever. As he handed the slip of paper across the desk, he said, "This will help with the pain." Sateesha took the prescription but felt puzzled. She thanked him and asked, "But what is my diagnosis?" She said the doctor looked uncomfortable and mumbled, "It looks like it's rheumatoid arthritis. My assistant will schedule a follow-up appointment." The physician might have felt compassion for the young woman. It's possible that he felt concern that her condition could affect her lifestyle and her employment. Yet, none of his care was expressed. Whatever he felt rendered him awkward and almost incoherent.

The owner of a bottling-plant franchise admitted that, at the prospect of having to terminate an employee, his feelings were overwhelming him. Adam told us,

> I can't stand this part of the business. I couldn't sleep all night
> and I have a pounding headache. I never know exactly what
> to say and whatever I do say comes out wrong. Then I watch
> their faces as they grasp the news, and in that moment I'm the
> enemy and there is nothing I can say that will make it better.

The owner has to learn to manage his emotions. He needs to balance his compassion with some pragmatic realization that hiring and firing are necessary aspects of running a business. He might find some relief in admitting some of his feelings to the employee. He could say directly, "I feel terrible having to let you go." If he has respect for the employee, he could voice it. "I respect your work ethic and the way that you contributed to the team. I will gladly write a letter of recommendation for you." Then, as honestly as he is able, he needs to provide the reason for the termination; for example, "I had to let five people go from your unit. Your position can be covered by others who have been here longer." He should be straightforward. He cannot erase the employee's emotions at the loss of her job. Trying to do so would be futile and probably irritating. He has to learn not to identify too much with the employee's emotions or to take personally her reaction. Terminating an employee is often a sad responsibility. The one bearing bad news can only try to temper its impact by honesty and by sensitivity. Some people actually exacerbate the receiver's emotional state by the hapless way in which they present the information.

A friend, Marty, declared that he was so furious with his lawyer that he slammed down the phone on her.

> We've been engaged in heated negotiations with a company that is trying to break a contract they have with us. My stupid lawyer called with this cheerful tone to tell me that the latest setback is good news. "It puts us in good position for the next go-round." Does she think I'm stupid? Why does she need to put spin on a lousy situation?

Why indeed? It's possible that the lawyer feared Marty's fury and didn't realize that by attempting to mitigate Marty's anger she was actually fueling it. The lawyer needs to speak the truth and resist attempting to manipulate Marty's emotions.

It's always a good rule of thumb to present bad news the way that you would appreciate receiving it. You would want to be notified truthfully, with respect and with consideration. One person recently shared with us intense feelings of irritation— not so much at the facts, but at the manner in which they were reported. Casey had been waiting for the delivery of a washing machine for two weeks after the day it had been promised. With laundry piled high, she was rankled by the distributor's words, "You have to be patient. Remember, once you get the machine you'll forget how long it took to get it. Like having a baby, ha, ha, ha."

Imparting bad news generates feelings in the speaker as well as in the one receiving the information. Unless the speaker addresses these feelings, the emotions can provoke unproductive behavior ranging from avoidance to defensiveness, inauthentic comments to silly clichés. Be mindful of the military axiom for delivering information, "Be accurate, be brief, and be clear"—and be humane.

## We Need to Talk Authentically in Our Roles

Keith is the newest member of the English department at a small college in New Hampshire. It's his first job after completing his master's degree, and his contract is only for the first semester. Keith truly wants to become a permanent member of the faculty. He and his wife love New Hampshire, and this college seems perfect for them. Fear of appearing inadequate has been keeping Keith from addressing a host of questions he has regarding students, curriculum, and course load. "I don't want anyone seeing me as insecure or unable to solve my own problems, so I'm reluctant to go to the chair of the department for information." Keith's frustration and fear are mounting as he encounters issues that could be settled readily by frank interaction with his peers or with the head of the department.

Keith needs to talk, but he has trapped himself in a young-professor role that does not allow him to be uninformed. In the role of the thoroughly prepared college instructor, he believes that he is expected to answer questions, not ask them. So he muddles through his first days and weeks, pretending to be familiar with policies and procedures. His uncertainty is self-imposed and unnecessary as he attempts to function without obtaining needed information. By failing to admit the truth, Keith becomes another self-fulfilling example of someone actually causing that which he fears—in this case, the appearance of insecurity.

We all have roles: director, manager, soldier, doctor, nurse, accountant, officer, teacher. Roles can enable us to do what we love to do: guide, educate, or provide treatment, protection, or service. Roles can free us to be who we aspire to be: one who loves, who preaches or teaches, who ministers or protects. Without being in the role of physician, an individual in our society would find it difficult to practice medicine. Unless someone is in the role of educator, his desire to teach would be difficult to realize. But for roles to empower us to be more completely ourselves, we have to define the role, not be defined by it. Keith will be fulfilled in his life-long ambition to be a professor if he defines what the role means for him. Does he want to do research or teach? Write or lecture? Spend his life learning knowledge or imparting it? Be solitary or part of an academic community? Keith is showing worrisome signs, however, of allowing the role to define him. He is becoming inauthentic by adapting his behavior to fulfill the expectations that he or others place on the role of professor. At the moment those expectations are leading him to suppress questions and feign cognizance. Unless he is alert to the temptation to *play* the role, he could soon be wearing a tweed jacket and riding a bike on campus to appear professorial.

Roles can stifle free and authentic expression. We conducted a seminar for rectors of Episcopal churches. A common complaint by the priests was their inability to express anger or even irritation and impatience in public. The role of rector, they asserted, doesn't permit such revelations of emotion; "Parishioners would be shocked." They discussed their awareness that their role model of authenticity, Christ, felt no such inhibition, yet that realization did not free them to be more real with their emotions. Additionally, they felt their roles as local pastors prevented them from saying no to parishioners' social invitations. They believed, and thought their parishioners believed, that they were expected to be always available. That lack of freedom led to small lies and evasions. Their reluctance to voice anger and to meet their personal needs led to depression, physical ailments, and, in some cases, dependence on alcohol.

Restrictive expectations attach themselves to all roles. Many parents feel required to be always available as chauffeurs, soccer moms, and cheering fans at every game. Teachers are not to be seen in bars. A soldier should be lean with short hair. Doctors have to be physically healthy, and nurses unflappable caregivers.

Recent television shows acquire their fascination by smashing role expectations, with a pill-popping nurse (Showtime's *Nurse Jackie*), an ill-tempered doctor (Fox's *House*), or an obsessive-compulsive detective (USA's *Monk*). Unless we are aware of the pull exerted by the roles we inhabit, we lose our freedom to say what we think and express what we feel.

It is gratifying for patients, students, and clients when professionals on whom they depend are able to be authentic while remaining highly competent in their professions. Our skilled dentist, after completing a complex procedure, told one of us, "I must apologize. I treated only your molar last week. That seemed to be the problem. You're back because there are cracks in your bicuspid that I overlooked. I regret the inconvenience for you." His candor was refreshing. Students have expressed admiration for teachers who answered questions by simply stating, "I'm not acquainted with that author," or, "I don't know the answer to your question. I'll look into it." A doctor we know, when commenting on the cause of the onset of symptoms said, "I'm afraid that will remain a mystery. I know no explanation for them." Some professionals have the security to admit ignorance. Some don't. A specialist answered a question we asked with a pompous, "The cause is idiopathic." Translated, his words merely mean, "I don't know." Insecure or arrogant individuals in all fields find it convenient to employ professional jargon. Their message is, "I know something that you don't," a message that hardly engenders trust or enhances interaction.

Communication can be complicated when individuals relate in more than one role. A physician speaks to her patient with authority in her office. When the patient is a friend or acquaintance or opponent on a tennis court, the doctor's authoritative tone is not so welcome. The doctor knows all parts of a patient's body, which is fine in his consulting room but can be awkward for the patient when they meet at coffee hour after Sunday service. An executive related his discomfort with dual roles:

> At work I try to be as open as possible with my boss. He has asked for my frankness, and I'm committed to providing it. But on his boat I feel wary. There are a lot of things I don't wish to discuss with him about me and my wife. But I get home and feel phony.

Some professionals avoid the complications of "wearing two hats" by deciding not to socialize with patients and clients. But that separation is not always easy or even desirable. Often, the professionals belong to the same temples or clubs as their clients. They live in the same neighborhoods, and their children go to the same schools. Whatever professional position you have, authenticity requires you to be aware of your needs and your feelings and to develop the freedom to set appropriate boundaries. The wise professional knows when to accept an invitation and when to decline, when to say yes and when to say no.

Professional roles are privileged positions that enable skilled individuals to touch others' lives on a regular basis. These persons can meet their patients, students, or clients in a profound manner that heals, teaches, and guides. The professional is invited into another person's life, often when the person is most vulnerable and most in need of authentic contact. Some will counsel the professional to be distant. A cynical older teacher advised Frank McCourt, the late author of *Angela's Ashes*, on how to behave as a teacher:

> Son, tell 'em nothing about yourself. You're the teacher. You have a right to privacy. The beggars are diabolical. They are not, repeat, not, your natural friends. You can never get back the bits and pieces of your life that stick in their little heads. Your life, man. It's all you have.

McCourt ignored the advice and became a personal hero to hundreds of students. Authentic professionals in classrooms and offices everywhere have a profound impact by taking the risk of being genuinely themselves.

## We Need to Talk, Even in Sensitive Situations

It is actually risky to be real. As you make yourself transparent, you open yourself to rejection. In hospitals, corporations, and classrooms, the danger has been magnified by a growing threat of lawsuits. Patient-advocacy groups have rightly put careless doctors and hospitals on notice that they must respect patients' rights and eschew shoddy care. A small percentage of physicians are responsible for botched procedures. But unfortunately, doctors as a group have grown defensive. Because of malpractice litigation, doctors are often advised to refrain even from apologizing to patients. Some teachers cherish their sacred trust of caring for the young, yet now many of these teachers are wary. Educators are warned to avoid any words that could be misunderstood as bullying or as unduly affectionate. A teacher at a workshop we were directing lamented her inability to hug a child who had fallen on the playground. Another described how a parent threatened to sue because she had told an overweight student in gym, "You've got to exercise more. You're getting too heavy for gymnastics." Police have to be trained not to abuse their power in enforcing the law. Attorney John L. Burris, in his seminal book *Blue vs. Black*, suggests a blueprint for police training, writing, "The critical need to teach effective communication skills cannot be stated often enough. It is the key to good policing. When misunderstanding or fear influences the interaction of the police with the commu-nity, force is usually substituted for reason." Some kinds of police work can easily provoke an adversarial reaction. Few people respond cheerily when stopped for speeding or told to get out of their car. The wise officer knows not to take resentment person-ally and certainly not to overreact to resistance.

Faced with antagonistic clientele, professionals can withdraw behind defensive shields. The consequence of taking a self-protective posture is less real contact for both the doctor with his patient and the teacher with her student. Concerns such as sexual harassment put restrictions on behavior in the workplace, but business, education, and the military are in danger of overreacting to the fear of lawsuits by creating an environment that promotes caution over spontaneity. Finding a balance that avoids inappropriate expression yet fosters mutual respect, trust, and freedom is the goal of responsible leaders.

## We Need to Talk to Relate with Difficult Individuals

No matter how skilled you may feel in your ability to communicate, you might be tested, possibly even defeated, by individuals with personalities you find trying. Here are a few examples of individuals in the workplace encountering personalities whose attitudes or behaviors range from unproductive to dangerous.

## *Arrogant Colleague*

A flight surgeon related to us an incident he experienced involving a senior helicopter pilot with a domineering personality. The surgeon described the basic tenet of cockpit interaction, called "positive communication." No one of the four crew members in a cockpit can see the full 360 degrees, so when an individual sights something potentially threatening, he alerts the pilot and the other crew members by saying, "Do you see what I'm seeing?" This is "positive communication," which calls for prompt acknowledgment from everyone in the cockpit. The pilot in this surgeon's story would pay no attention to these alerts. He dismissed the observations with, "Get a grip," "Get real," or some such dismissive remark. The surgeon confronted the pilot with his concern about the dangers posed by this behavior. The pilot rebuffed him in an arrogant tone, "Doc, I don't tell you how to practice medicine. You don't tell me how to fly."

The surgeon had confronted what he perceived as irresponsible, dangerous behavior, but was rebuffed. Many of us in a parallel position would have failed to speak up, at least directly, to the person involved. The surgeon could have talked about the pilot to others who he was confident would agree with him. He could have criticized the pilot to the men who flew with him, either to show sympathy or to win their approval. In so doing, he would have done nothing to correct reckless behavior, while probably causing further harm to crew morale. Gossip and carping are no more productive in military settings than they are in an office or in the home.

The surgeon spoke forthrightly to the pilot, the one who could potentially learn from his remarks, and was not stopped by a snub or satisfied that he had done what he could. When he continued to observe the senior pilot making up his own procedures that the surgeon perceived as further destroying morale and endangering the lives of the crew, he spoke forcefully to the commanding officer. When the commander was hesitant to intervene, the flight surgeon courageously stated that unless action was taken he would ground all crews by declaring them "medically non-adaptable" for flight. The commander relented. With the assistance of a chaplain skilled in communication, the surgeon immediately inaugurated a program that brought crew members and senior pilots together for communication sessions in which rank was put aside and totally frank discussion was expected. This honest, responsible surgeon cared enough about company safety and morale to speak up and to keep speaking up until he made a difference.

When you encounter a colleague or client who is harmfully dismissive of you or others, your confidence and even your courage might be tested. A productive way to proceed could include the following steps:

- Identify your needs or feelings regarding this individual.

- Clarify your perceptions of the behavior that you regard as non-receptive to you, your ideas, or those of others.

- Ask yourself whether you can imagine a satisfying encounter with the individual.

- Consider whether you might need an intermediary, for instance, someone in the human resources department.

- Choose a course of action.

Don't waste energy complaining about the issue to individuals who cannot effect change, and don't exhaust yourself obsessing about the behavior that offends you. If you decide to speak to the person directly, avoid aggression and be specific about your feelings, perceptions, and needs. If he or she rejects your effort, don't be discouraged. If you have recourse to a superior who could be helpful, consider speaking up. Try not to let this individual become a preoccupation or an encumbrance on your peace of mind and performance.

## Angry Customer

An angry customer stared at the store employee and said, "Please explain why this part isn't covered by the warranty." The employee countered, "If you're not happy with our work, maybe you ought to take your computer somewhere else." The customer responded, "I've already spent a lot of money here, and I just want to know why this part isn't covered." The employee reacted, "You should have read your warranty. We included it with your computer purchase. There's nothing else we can do." The customer insisted, "I did read it. I'm asking you to explain it to me." Again, the store clerk repeated, "If you had read the warranty you would understand it. We can't do anything more." At that, the customer stormed out of the shop.

The employee turned an angry customer into a furious one. He lost an opportunity to communicate effectively and lost a customer. He could have responded to the situation constructively, resulting in understanding between store clerk and customer. Instead, he reacted in a way guaranteed to produce a belligerent standoff. In order to meet the customer in a satisfying manner, the clerk needed to have been aware of his feelings as well as the customer's.

The clerk might have felt a number of emotions:

■ Anxiety at encountering the customer's anger.

■ Defensiveness regarding his store and the warranty.

■ Resentment at being spoken to in anger.

He might have felt any number of other feelings that had nothing to do with the incident but were due to events that happened earlier in the day or at home.

The customer might have felt a number of emotions, as well:

■ Frustration that his computer was malfunctioning again.

■ Fear that he had no funds to pay for fixing the computer.

■ Anger that the warranty seemed bogus.

Also, the customer might have felt any number of unrelated emotions, prompted by having received a speeding ticket on the way to the store, or having had an argument with his son who has failing grades, or having heard that he owes more taxes. Knowing his own feelings, the clerk could have prevented them from coloring his response to the customer. Instead, he immediately reacted aggressively by encouraging the customer to go elsewhere. He could have tried to put himself in the shoes of the customer and shown sympathy for the predicament. "I know that it has to be frustrating when you believe that the warranty is going to cover all the costs and then it doesn't." Often an individual will temper the tone of his complaint if he experiences even a modicum of understanding.

The salesperson who listens, who doesn't take a customer's feelings personally, and who knows his own feelings can defuse a customer's anger. Maybe the customer is not always right, but he does deserve to be met respectfully. His anger doesn't have to classify him as the enemy to be defended against or attacked.

You will surely encounter angry individuals at work. Take care that you do not meet fire with fire. Know and learn to control the feelings their anger provokes within you. Don't react. Often behind their anger are other feelings such as hurt or fear. Try to listen and to understand. Sometimes you need to be tolerant and accepting of their forceful feelings. At other times you need to respond by establishing self-respecting boundaries. You have to balance their freedom to emote with your need for respect. If you choose to address these individuals directly about their anger, avoid blame and judgment. State the effect their anger is having on you, and articulate your need for less volatile discussion. Don't act the victim or patronize. Be honest.

> Often an individual will temper the tone of his complaint if he experiences even a modicum of understanding.

## Competitive Colleague

Glen joined an information-technology consulting company knowing fully that it was a highly competitive firm. What he didn't expect was the intensity of competition among his colleagues. He dived into the first project he was assigned and enthusiastically co-wrote a program with his team member, Denzel. Together, they spent long hours making the program run smoothly, knowing it would save their client money and time. One afternoon, Glen became angry when he heard his coworker talking about the program and claiming full credit for its unique solutions to complicated information technology demands. When Glen confronted his partner, Denzel defended himself, saying, "Everyone knows we both worked on it. The client will know your part." Glen backed off, but learned later that he would not be participating in the formal presentation of the program to their client.

The news hit Glen like a punch. Anger, hurt, distrust, and disillusionment were some of the feelings he registered. He knew himself enough to avoid reacting in an explosive manner on the job. Privately, in difficult moments, he imagined quitting his new job, slamming his partner against his desk, or calling him a "slimeball" and worse. Instead, the path Glen chose to follow serves as a paradigm of mature response. He began by talking over his options with his wife, Lena. He reflected on three courses of action:

1. He could confront Denzel powerfully but with self-control, saying, "I'm angry that you would take full credit for our work. If I let this stand, I would resent you and never want to partner with you again. That would be bad all the way around. So I want you to talk to Wally (their boss) and let him know how we worked together and what each of us contributed; then let him decide where we go from there about the presentation. If you won't do that, I will talk to him alone."

Glen was aware that this path was his preference, but it had risks. He could alienate a coworker who had been with the firm much longer than he had. He might offend Wally, who had chosen Denzel to make the client presentation. He could appear as a whiner needing attention.

2. He could go to Wally directly. Since he had already confronted Denzel to no avail, Glen could skip another futile interaction and make his case to the person he was reporting to, Wally.

Glen knew the downside of this option was that Wally would probably need to call Denzel into the meeting anyway in order to allow both men to speak. Wally could regard Glen as immature and not able to stand up for himself. Besides, Wally might have a special relationship with Denzel and be unreceptive to Glen's observations.

3. He could decide to accept the situation, say nothing, and allow the quality of his work to be known in time.

Glen knew that the third option could make him appear weak to Denzel, and possibly to Wally, and might stimulate in himself feelings of resentment and distrust not only toward Denzel but also toward Wally and even the company.

After much reflection and discussion with his wife, Glen resolved that "prudence was the better part of valor." Since he was new to the firm and not yet thoroughly familiar with its culture, for the moment he would say nothing to Wally. He did decide, however, to share his feelings of anger with Denzel. He kept his remarks brief, didn't react to Denzel's defensiveness, and stated clearly that if the situation recurred, his reaction would be far less tolerant. He felt honest, in control, and self-respecting.

Like Glen, you deserve to receive credit when credit is due. It is not childish to want recognition for your work. Some people deny that need. They expect little attention and tend to receive what they expect. "An honest day's pay for an honest day's work" is a healthy maxim for which the psychological counterpart could be, "An honest acknowledgement for an honest job." If a coworker tries to steal that merited recognition, your feelings of resentment, hurt, or disappointment demonstrate not only that you expect due affirmation but also that you expect fair play from a colleague. If you choose to confront your colleague, don't get stuck pointing the finger at the unprincipled behavior. Rather, voice your feelings such as resentment and your need not only for credit but also for trust so that you can work collaboratively with your colleagues.

### Moody Supervisor

A group of young accountants discussed their moody boss, Stuart. They are smart, creative, and energetic. Their company is small but growing rapidly. A fresh-faced young woman remarked, "When we get together we seem to charge each other's batteries. We can see problems from different angles, critique one another's ideas, and come together on a joint solution. But Stuart comes in and we go quiet." A male colleague added, "We're guarded, very careful with what we say." Another said, "We have to be. You never know what mood he'll be in. Mostly he is negative—so pessimistic that any new approach will work. Sometimes he lightens up, but he can go dark fast. Then he is witheringly critical." Another commented, "He must be liked by senior management. I wonder if he's as negative with them."

After further discussion, they acknowledged that they had begun to complain too much to one another about their boss. His moods had actually started to dominate their own. They themselves were becoming negative, saying in one way or another, "We can't be ourselves or do what we are capable of with Stuart as a boss." They were absorbing his mood and blaming him for their guardedness. They discussed their reluctance to speak freely in his presence and their frustration with themselves for failing to submit their ideas for his scrutiny. It didn't take long for these talented people to realize that their attitude and behavior were not satisfying for them nor fruitful for the company. They resolved to focus less on Stuart's words and more on their own courage to speak up confidently. Instead of being controlled by his moods, perhaps they could influence him with their enthusiasm. And even if he didn't change, they could be more vocal. A boss does have the power to create an atmosphere, but the young accountants internalized our maxim: "An immature person relies on his environment; a mature person creates it."

The young advertising accountants learned to relate to a moody boss by understanding themselves. An executive in the fashion business discovered how to cope with his moody boss by learning more about her. He told us,

> I think I understand that she just needs to think by herself before she makes a move. I used to think she was odd, but I understand now that she's just different from me. I need to talk things out and get everyone's feedback. First she reads, thinks, reflects, but then she always comes back with a thoughtful answer. It took me awhile to realize she wasn't avoiding or withdrawing or even moody.

This executive learned what all of us who tend to judge need to realize: labeling another person doesn't usually foster understanding. Instead of judging, we have to acknowledge how the other person impacts us and then take responsibility for our response. Certainly some individuals act in ways that appear arrogant, self-serving, or angry. The challenge for each of us is to respond to these persons as authentically as we are able. Merely judging them and reacting to them with blame, aggression, submission, or avoidance accomplishes nothing productive.

A cynical colleague or boss can poison the atmosphere at work. His or her emotional state can seep into yours and threaten your sense of well-being. Identify how you are affected. Do you try to placate or avoid the other's mood, or try to balance it by projecting an opposite mood? Do you join your colleague by matching his critical, skeptical, or negative attitude with your own? After examining your reactions, try to imagine how you want to act in spite of the other's words. Resolve to be yourself more freely. You could also choose to inform your colleague about the effect his moods have on you. If you decide to speak up, try not to blame, but simply relate your difficulty in being as cheerful or candid as you would like to be in the presence of his brooding behavior.

## We Need to Talk to Manage Effectively

Raymond is a highly respected manager at a large financial-services firm in Los Angeles. We gathered a cross section of men and women who report to him, in order to assess their views on what makes Raymond successful. Their answers not only identify the reasons they believe Raymond is effective, but they also depict concretely the qualities of a good manager. Some stressed the clarity of his direction:

- "You always know what he wants. He sets out the goal and describes the objectives that have to be met to reach it. With some bosses, you never know for sure where they are going or where they want us to go."

- "I agree. That's why morale is good here. We work together. He points the way—very clear!"

- "That's how he motivates. He defines the goal of any project and explains why it's the goal, how we can meet it, and when."

■ "He spells out each of our roles, so we know who is doing what."

Others in the group focused on his attitude:

■ "Ray is very positive. I can be feeling down or skeptical, but he has this contagious positive attitude."

■ "That's true, but he isn't all rah-rah. He's realistic. He listens to objections and is willing to modify his ideas."

■ "He cares about us. I know I'm not the only one he has asked, 'Where do you want to go in the company? What are your personal goals?' Some managers are all ego. Ray isn't."

Some talked about his direct communication:

■ "Ray lets you know if he doesn't like what you're doing. He's not sarcastic or mean, just direct and honest. I appreciate that."

■ "He'll also say, 'Good job.' He texted me once on a weekend to compliment me on work I did."

The group respected Ray for the way that he interacted with them. Several remarked that he was available, that "he gets out on the floor and talks to us." They credited their morale and personal motivation to his clear, caring communication.

We also talked to Cliff, another manager in the same company who was experiencing some difficulty motivating a few of his team. He spoke of a middle-aged sales trader who had recently returned from a sick leave. "I hired her to bring experience to a team that is composed of young guys. She was productive for a while but now is not measuring up." We asked what he planned to say to her. "I'm going to be blunt: 'You've got just thirty days to produce or you're gone.'" We urged that, instead of issuing such a dire threat, he tell her clearly what he needs from her. After some reflection and discussion he decided to say to her,

> Caroline, you've been through a tough time, but now I need you to meet the purpose I hired you for. Here are the areas that I need you to focus on: Be available to mentor some of

the younger guys. Be an example to them of diligent, responsible performance. Produce at the level you did shortly after I hired you. Report to me each Tuesday at the 8:00 a.m. meeting so that I know the results of the past week and your objectives for the coming week. Finally, I need to know that you're committed to these changes.

Cliff commented, "This really helps. I had to know what I needed from her and state the needs clearly. I didn't want to threaten her, but I did need to see results. So that's what I have to do—tell her that. Tell her what I need." Managers need to talk to provide leadership. They have to know where they want to take the group and then they have to motivate, challenge, and guide with clear communication.

Most of us spend more waking hours at work than at home. Sometimes we interact more with coworkers and colleagues than we do with our family members. So our lives are considerably enhanced or stressed by our work environment. We can look forward to going to work in a setting in which we are free to be creative, or we can dread entering a work space in which we are on guard. We can thrive in a setting that encourages cooperation, collaboration, and teamwork, or be threatened in one that is overly competitive, marked by an everyone-for-himself ethos.

The *toxic environment* promotes damaging dos and don'ts:

- Don't share information that might make someone else look good.

- Don't show your hand or admit vulnerability or doubt.

- Don't compliment anyone.

- Don't encourage.

- Don't comfort.

- Do blame others to advance yourself.

- Do judge others to appear superior.

- Do criticize others to have the upper hand.

- Do threaten others to keep them where you want them.

The *productive atmosphere*, on the other hand, encourages you to act more positively:

- Trust your colleagues.

- Act in a trustworthy manner.

- Treat your colleagues as you wish to be treated.

- Communicate openly and honestly.

- Be generous with your praise.

- Be constructive with your criticism.

- Be available to help.

- Be self-respecting in establishing boundaries.

- Be open to suggestions.

- Be clear in your directives.

- Be prepared for meetings.

- Be faithful to your responsibilities.

- Meet your own needs.

In this healthy environment, you don't waste time and energy in futile, distrustful conflict but function at your optimum level, being, as the old Army ads promise, "all that you can be."

### ■ FOR REFLECTION ■

1. Do you know how you express yourself so that people can trust you?

2. At work, when and with whom are you fearful of speaking up?

3. When have you had to deliver bad news? Do you think you imparted the information accurately, clearly, succinctly, and humanely?

4. Are you authentic in your work role, or do you become less yourself and less open at work than you are in other parts of your life?

5. Are there people at work with whom you find it difficult to communicate? Do you know why?

Chapter Five

# *talking among friends*

You just call out my name and you know
wherever I am
I'll come running to see you again.

—Carole King, "You've Got a Friend"

In her book *No Ordinary Time*, the historian Doris Kearns
Goodwin describes the characteristics and influence of friendship while depicting the relationship that Eleanor Roosevelt
enjoyed with the reporter Lorena "Hick" Hickok:

> There is every evidence that Hick's love for Eleanor came at
> a critical moment in Eleanor's life, providing a mix of ten-
> derness, loyalty, confidence, and courage that sustained her
> in her struggle to redefine her sense of self and her position
> in the world. For Eleanor, Hick's love was a positive force
> allowing her to grow and to take wing, write the story of her
> life the way she wanted it to be, even in the White House.
> Secure in the knowledge that she was loved by the most
> important woman in her life, Eleanor was able to create a
> public persona that was to earn the love of millions. Eleanor
> wrote to Hick, "You taught me more than you know and it
> brought me happiness. . . . You made of me so much more of
> a person. . . ."

We seek friendships to meet our needs for companionship, warmth, and support. Families are given to us; friendships we choose. As the proverb proclaims, "A good friend is my nearest relation." In Roosevelt and Hickok's relationship, each of these brilliant women had been rejected or neglected by relatives, spouses, or partners. In friendship, they were able to talk confidently, trusting that they and what they shared would receive loving attention. Friendship can meet needs we have for someone to play with or someone to pursue a goal with; but, whether we play or plan, friendship provides us someone to talk with.

> Friendship allows a secure zone for self-revelation, free from the compli-cated influences of blood bonds or the tensions of sexual, romantic relationships.

Goodwin writes, "Hick told Eleanor the story of her childhood days on a poor dairy farm 'with an abusive father.' Hick's story touched Eleanor profoundly, prompting her to share with the reporter the story of her own wretched childhood." Each of the friends was safe to disclose herself without fear of judgment. There were many people around Roosevelt, including her husband, the president, with whom she did not feel safe to reveal past or present experiences. Like Eleanor Roosevelt, we need to talk openly without fear, and a friend is often one with whom we choose to disclose ourselves—what we did and felt yesterday and today. Friendship allows a secure zone for self-revelation, free from the complicated influences of blood bonds or the tensions of sexual, romantic relationships.

## We Need to Talk about Ourselves to a Friend

Boasting is annoying to the person having to listen. Self-absorbed monologues are obnoxious. These egotistical presentations give talking about oneself a bad name. But, unquestionably, you do need to talk about yourself. You need to talk for the fun of sharing your experiences or for the opportunity to clarify your thoughts. From infancy, you come to know yourself by putting yourself into words. And friends sharing themselves nourish their friendships.

Brandon, a high school teacher, recalled meeting with an old friend:

> I picked Carl up at the airport to take him to our twentieth high school reunion. We had been good friends during our teenage years, but hadn't seen each other much since graduation. As we drove along, we caught up on our marriages, children, and work. When I remarked, "I would never have predicted you to be a social worker. You didn't even want to go to school." Carl mused, "I know. Boy, I hated school. I'll tell you how it changed for me. A couple of years after we graduated I went to a community college in Denver where I'd been skiing. Then I joined the Peace Corps. It changed my life. I saw poverty like you wouldn't believe." Carl told me his story while the traffic was jammed up all the way to the reunion. When we finally pulled into the hotel parking lot, Carl remarked, "My wife knows bits and pieces of that story, but I've never told the whole thing from high school to today. I hope it was entertaining." "Are you kidding?" I remarked, "That was fascinating—like listening to a book on tape."

Evidently, Carl was pleased to talk about himself. He needed a friend who was interested. Also, he might have needed a captive audience and the intimate setting provided by a car in heavy traffic. They could have driven in silence or listened to music. But, as old friends, they wanted to learn about one another and to talk about their lives.

Phyllis, an elementary school teacher, talked about a special encounter she had with a friend:

> I was sitting on a bench outside of my church. A very dear friend saw me and noticed that I was crying. She sat down beside me and held my hand. I talked about reflections I'd had about the readings of the day. They had tapped tender thoughts I had had about forgiveness. I told her that I've always wondered if I really ever have "forgiven and forgotten." I have so many regrets about not letting go of a lot of things with my parents. I held on too long to little resentments.

Phyllis continued, "I was so grateful to her. I had painful and somewhat shameful thoughts, yet I was able to share them. Evidently I trusted her more than I knew." Phyllis, like Carl, needed to talk to someone she trusted. Sometimes your spouse or a sibling or a cousin is your best friend with whom you share everything—your hurts, joys, interests. But your life is enhanced by having others, old and new friends, with whom you can talk about your life.

When a friend shares his or her doubts and fears, and recounts personal missteps, you realize that you are not alone in your faults and in your self-recrimination. Thoughts that seemed bizarre when hurtling inside your mind appear less weird when you listen to a trusted friend voice similar ideas. With a friend you can divulge your thoughts, bring them into the light of day, and see them more clearly. You can say, "Let me run this idea past you," and trust that the interaction will keep you tethered to reality. Talking about yourself with a friend helps you to know yourself, enables you to understand your friend, and draws you and your friend closer.

All of us instinctively resist looking weak or flawed. We want to be admired and respected, and we fear being seen as deficient. Frans de Waal, the zoologist and author of *Peacemaking Among Primates*, points out that men in particular, like their male primate counterparts, avoid appearing vulnerable. According to de Waal, they fear being at a competitive disadvantage with other males. He writes, "Perhaps males always feel surrounded by others hoping for them to stumble." The fear of being vulnerable interpersonally, however, is not reserved to males. None of us, male or female, wants to be hurt or have our vulnerability exploited. Yet we all have doubts about ourselves. We need to share these feelings, but in doing so we risk being misunderstood and having our admission of weakness exploited. As one woman admitted to us, "I can't admit any mistake I make to him. He'll throw it in my face the next time we argue." She yearned to let down her guard with her husband, but shuddered at the peril of doing so.

We all want to voice our anxieties and air our limitations. We want to confess our misdeeds and foibles. But we need to trust that we will not lose love or respect by being truthful, and we need to believe that what we share in private will not be repeated in public. We need a good friend with whom we can be completely frank.

## We Need to Talk Freely to Explore Issues

Ralph Waldo Emerson writes, "A friend is a person with whom I may be sincere. Before him I may think aloud." Like Emerson, we need friends with whom we have unfettered freedom to put our thoughts into words. With these friends we don't need to have reached solid conclusions or to have forged foolproof arguments. We can expose a thought or experiment with an idea.

Veronica was penitent in therapy as she related becoming attracted to a married man at a convention. "I know it's wrong. There's nowhere to go with this. He's married. But it is so hard to let go. I'm thinking about him all the time." Veronica continued to cry and to talk about the powerful attraction she felt toward the man. Then she said,

> Thank God I have such a good friend in Rosie. I can tell her anything. I can lay out all my temptations: to text him, to call him to see if he's feeling what I am, to arrange to meet him. She knows, and I know, that I've got to let go. She listens. Then she tells me, "You can do it. Do not call him." Without her to talk to I think I'd go nuts.

Sometimes you want to explore your thoughts, dreams, and possibilities with someone who will not panic, judge, or burden you with warnings or advice. A good friend at these times is a godsend. Leroy, a successful mortgage broker, pondered the benefits of friendship, saying, "I'd love to be able to discuss with my wife all the pros and cons of changing careers, even moving out west, but she would freak. I had a roommate in college I could talk to about anything. I don't have a good friend like that now. I could use one." A college student echoed Leroy's plight. "I want to talk through whether law school is really for me. Maybe there's something else I'd like to get into, like journalism, or just taking some time after graduation to see what I want to do. But my dad won't begin to hear me. He's a lawyer and law is what's best for me—according to him. He's paying, so what can I do?"

Dad, with his agenda, is not the one to whom this young man turns to help sort out his future. He needs to talk, to give free rein to his imagination, to explore his needs, talents, and passions. He needs a friend. The time to talk to his dad is after he has clarified his thoughts, not before he has had space to examine them. Young people need to talk to friends to discover themselves, their values, opinions, and interests. So do we all.

## We Need to Talk about Our Interests

In a delightful movie, *The Girl in the Café*, a young woman asks a male character who has a high position in the British Chancellor's office to tell her about a complicated government issue. He fears she will be bored. "No," she says, "I won't. Tell me." As soon as he starts, she drops her head and feigns sleep; they share a laugh. But it is not funny when what interests us bores our listener. We need a friend or group of friends with whom we can discuss gardening or wrestling, stamp collecting or baseball, politics or cooking. Sometimes the shared interest leads to a more profound friendship and the kind of talking that deepens the relationship. Rabbi Marc Gellman writes about playing golf with his best friend, Monsignor Thomas Hartman. "The hours Tommy and I spent on the course were golden and precious in maintaining our friendship. Whether we were talking about a golf shot or about the world didn't matter. We were talking and laughing and learning."

Another golfer, Richard M. Smith, chairman and editor in chief of *Newsweek*, met Mark Vittert of St. Louis on a course in Michigan. Together they began to play marathon matches, which never averaged less than thirty-six holes in a day. Smith writes in *Golf Digest*,

> No surprise, we've become the best of friends. What do we talk about? The short answer is "everything." We're both deeply interested in business, politics, and the media, but we're every bit as likely to talk about our families or the mysteries of a flop shot.

This shared interest in golf became a vehicle for deepening their relationship, but a friendship can sputter and die when interests are not shared. A mother described watching her son try to build a friendship:

> A family moved in next door. The couple has a son our son's age. I was so hopeful they would be friends. They have tried to get together but it's not working. My son wants to play basketball all the time and this little neighbor is just not interested in sports.

With friends you can do what interests you and talk about these interests. Some friends go to concerts and talk about music, some hunt or fish and tell stories of the "one that got away," and some delight in sharing gardening tips. You want to discuss your interests with friends who "get it."

## We Need to Talk to Reach a Common Goal

In his memoirs, Winston Churchill described his friendship with Harry Hopkins, President Roosevelt's trusted advisor. Churchill knew that the outcome of World War II would depend on the support and help of the United States. In 1941, Roosevelt sent Hopkins to England to meet with Churchill to assess personally Britain's resolve and needs. Churchill huddled privately with Hopkins for hours, laying out his nation's entire state of affairs. Churchill writes, "And from this hour began a friendship between us which sailed serenely over all earthquakes and convulsions. He was the most perfect channel of communication between the president and me." Churchill attributed victory to their friendship and to Hopkins's "refined comprehension of the Cause. It was to be the defeat, ruin, and slaughter of Hitler." According to Doris Kearns Goodwin, the prime minister's friendship with Roosevelt himself was not as serene, but was an essential bond in their joint enterprise of winning the war. Before D-Day, Churchill wrote to the president, "Our friendship is my greatest standby amid the ever-increasing complication of this exacting war." These great men needed to talk bluntly and to confide trustingly to one another to accomplish their common goal.

Two men born in a different generation and involved in entertaining people rather than saving them had the same need to talk. Frankie Valli and Bob Gaudio were founding members of the singing group The Four Seasons. Gaudio decided he no longer wanted to sing with the group but rather wanted to write their songs full time. He feared, though, that this activity could have significant costs: loss of identification as one of the group, loss of recognition, and loss of financial rewards. Valli and Gaudio talked and the result of their frank discussion, made famous in the musical *The Jersey Boys*, was the "the Jersey handshake." With a handshake, the two musicians sealed a financial agreement that has lasted decades. Their friendship and common background provided the foundation of trust that made their discussion and agreement possible.

Ben Cohen and Jerry Greenfield were self-acknowledged chubby pals in junior high school. They both loved to eat and demonstrated their love of food by creating the Clean Plate Club in the cafeteria at school. After going their separate ways to college, they reunited in 1977 to start a business together. With their enjoyment of eating, they decided that the enterprise had to involve food. Their first idea was to found UBS, United Bagel Service. They dropped that idea in favor of making and selling ice cream. Ben and Jerry's eventually became a $100-million, publicly held company. While building their company, the two friends talked for hours about their shared value of social responsibility. They wanted their employees to feel cared for and listened to. They wanted a family feel to their company and were committed to a business that gave back to the community. They decided to allocate 7.5 percent of pre-tax profits to socially responsible programs. These two old friends talked their way into discovering their desire to work together, producing the kind of business that would feed their enthusiasm, and forming the familial and socially committed spirit that would imbue it.

Friendships can expand when friends share a common project: designing a memory album, building a model plane, or organizing a charity event. Working together, friends learn about one another's creativity, pace, doggedness, generosity, and sensitivities. They talk to establish goals and to solve problems. They talk to set strategies and make decisions. Children learn many social skills by playing games with friends. As adults, we continue learning about ourselves and our friends as we discuss options and negotiate differences while working together to achieve shared goals.

## We Need to Talk When Friendships Go Wrong

A Chinese proverb advises, "Do not use a hatchet to remove a fly from a friend's forehead." Another piece of wisdom warns, "Don't turn a blind eye to a friend's self-destructive behavior." A friend who is bent on a harmful path doesn't need to be pummeled, but might well need to be confronted. A young man we saw in therapy stubbornly denied all evidence that he was abusing alcohol, drugs, and himself. Then a long-time friend told him that they could no longer be friends and that he was not welcome to visit the family until he "stopped living like a jerk." The words of the forthright friend had the salutary influence that months of therapy had failed to provide.

The woman we described earlier who was obsessing about a possible affair with a married man needed the strength of her friend saying, "Don't pick up the phone." We have heard grateful testimonials to friends who took the risk to speak up on difficult topics. "He made me aware of how I was treating my wife." "They expressed their disappointment at my continually being late." "He wouldn't let me drive after a night of partying." "She reminded me that I was ignoring my middle child."

> A friend who is bent on a harmful path doesn't need to be pummeled, but might well need to be confronted.

Good friendships are not always serene. A friend can feel exploited or taken for granted. As Fred Lager describes in *Ben & Jerry's: The Inside Scoop*, resentment at perceived unfairness erupted between the old friends and business partners.

> One day, Ben was helping Jerry package some Oreo Mint, and every single pint was filling up halfway, which was driving Jerry crazy. They were making batch after batch, and essentially filling every pint by hand with the spoon. Finally, Jerry burst out, "There's no way I'm gonna keep doing this, Ben. I've had it." "Hey, I'm just out there on the truck every

day, breaking down all over the place. I don't have it easy either, you know," Ben shot back. It was rare for the two life-long friends to be at odds over anything to the point where either raised his voice. Jerry backed down immediately, acknowledging that Ben was putting up with just as much crap in doing his job as Jerry was in doing his. Jerry put the incident into an optimistic perspective, "It'll be a big scene in the movie," he predicted.

Good friends want you to be a good spouse, parent, and person. You need their example and their words to remind you and motivate you to be what you yourself want to be. A good friend finds the right moment and the right words to confront, remind, and invite you to be your best self. That friend is able to be tolerant, forgiving, and accepting, but also has the courage to tell you kindly what you need to know.

## We Need to Talk about Our Values

Arturo is a recovering alcoholic. He described Alcoholics Anonymous (AA) as a major influence in his resolve to be sober. It provides a setting where individuals are able to talk about what they value and inspire other members with what they say.

> I went to a meeting to check out AA, to see if it would help. There was a guy talking about the serenity he had found in his life after years of anxiety. What he said started me feeling peaceful. I wanted what he had. I told him that last week on my fifth anniversary of sobriety.

Friends have a significant influence on one another as they reveal their values to each other. Ben Cohen and Jerry Greenfield strengthened one another's social conscience. A fellow AA member's regard for serenity stirred Arturo in his own search for peace. Hick's conviction of the importance of journalism led Eleanor to write her enormously popular syndicated column, "My Day." Friends have been led to enjoy opera, bible study, science fiction, or growing bonsai trees because a friend talked about the subject with enthusiasm. A study in the *New England Journal of Medicine* demonstrates that friends exert such influence on one another that a heavier person tends to eat less when with lean friends than with heavier ones. Parents attempting to steer their children from the wrong crowd have known forever the influence of friends. The novelist Cervantes writes, "Tell me the company thou keepst, and I'll tell thee what thou art."

As members of AA and many religious communities affirm, friends have a responsibility to one another.

> A good friend finds the right moment and the right words to confront, remind, and invite you to be your best self.

We mentioned earlier in the book, and demonstrate later, that all of us at one time or another need courage to confront one another with constructive criticism. Friends surely have that charge; however, friends exert an even more profound effect on one another's lives by their lived values.

Having a friend who thinks of you, likes you, needs you, and wants to talk with you gives you a sense of well-being. All of us struggle to feel that we are worthwhile. Yet, without friends it is extremely challenging to appreciate ourselves, to believe that we are lovable. At one time or another, we are all slighted, buffeted, ignored, or rejected in ways that contribute to our self-doubt. But when we turn to the safety of a friendship to talk, to be heard, and to be encouraged, we are validated and bolstered in self-esteem.

## ■ FOR REFLECTION ■

1. Can you describe a time when sharing with a friend was particularly satisfying?

2. What about this friendship created a "safe zone" for talking?

3. Is there a way you communicate that interferes with developing friendships?

4. Do you have particular interests that developed because they were shared with a friend?

5. Is there a value that has become more meaningful to you because it was affirmed by a friend?

# you don't want
# to talk
# this way

# Chapter Six

# *all the ways we don't say
what we mean*

Yes, we think of things that matter,
With words that must be said,
"Can analysis be worthwhile?"
"Is the theater really dead?"
And how the room is softly faded
And I only kiss your shadow,
I cannot feel your hand,
You're a stranger now unto me
Lost in the dangling conversation
And the superficial sighs
In the borders of our lives.

—Paul Simon, "The Dangling Conversation"

## Indirect, Ineffective Forms of Expression

If words were made for talking, and talking was meant for connecting us to others, why in the world have we developed so
many ways to talk that keep us apart? We have the power
through words to reveal ourselves—
our thoughts, insights, experiences,
emotions, needs, yearnings, hopes, and
dreams. We can talk to make ourselves
known, seen, and trusted. We can
bridge the space between ourselves
and others with words. With words we
can divulge the mystery of who we are and come to know the
unique story of another person. Yet we suffer and we cause others to suffer when, instead of talking to reveal ourselves to
another, we talk to hide and withhold ourselves.

> We talk in ways
> that create distrust
> not trust, distance
> not closeness.

We talk in ways that create distrust not trust, distance not
closeness. Most of the time we do this unproductive talking
unwittingly. We develop habits of speaking that don't meet our
need to be known, that don't present who we really are or even
what we really mean. Before we can learn skills of effective communication, we have to recognize these habits of ineffective
communication and become more quickly aware of them as we
speak so that we can stop them.

So, what bad habits of verbal communication do you have?
Some common forms of inauthentic, ineffective expression include:

- Speaking impersonally—saying "you" or "one" when you
  mean "I."

- Asking questions—questions hide the one asking while
  expecting the other to express him- or herself.

- Withholding yourself—staying invisible by keeping silent.

- Fibbing, evading, and exaggerating—either refusing to tell
  the truth or putting your spin on the facts.

- Judging—instead of sharing yourself, you label others.

- Blaming, threatening, and giving ultimatums—focusing
  critical pressure on others, forcing them to change, or else.

■ Using absolutes, universals, and intellectualizations—saying words like "never" and "always" and hiding feelings behind heady language.

■ Talking sarcastically and facetiously or using humor to avoid expressing your feelings.

We examine each of these modes of expression in the ensuing chapters. You might be inclined to defend these modes of expression. You might even defend them while employing ineffective speech. "*Everyone* judges. *You* have to!" What these unproductive communication habits have in common is that they excuse you from having to speak personally. They excuse you from revealing your own emotion and stating your own opinion truthfully. In effect, they veil the real you behind words that don't require you to be visible.

## Remaining Silent or Exaggerating

Why is admitting what you feel, need, think, and have done so difficult? You want to be known and seen, understood and loved. Your words can make you visible and therefore make being known possible. But survival is a primal human instinct. Revealing yourself potentially opens you to hurt from misunderstanding, criticism, rejection, and even ridicule. The heroic priest Father Mychal Judge served as a chaplain to the New York Fire Department and was killed on 9/11 at the World Trade Center. He was revered by the firemen, known to President Bush and First Lady Laura Bush, and befriended by two mayors of the city. Yet, according to his close friends, he lived in "purgatory," fearing that if he admitted his gay sexual orientation, his firemen friends would reject him. In another example of fear hindering transparency and the open revelation of self, a woman described to us her oppressive sense of isolation as she coped with her teenage son's troubles with the police, the courts, and teachers. "I would so like to tell my mother and family who live in Europe. I just was over there visiting and I couldn't say anything. I don't know why. I guess it is shame."

Fr. Mychal and this mother, like all of us, don't want to be hurt. Like them, instead of being fully open we tend to cover and even disguise ourselves. Words behave as camouflage. We become opaque rather than transparent. Those who love us have to speculate on who we are, what we think, and how we feel.

Examine the way that you talk. You might discover that you find it less risky to speak impersonally, and so you often focus on the weather rather than on yourself. You may hide behind questions that don't require you to expose yourself, or you may use humor to avoid saying anything about yourself at all. Yet these strategies don't work. They won't resolve your vulnerability and can even leave you feeling alone. Like many people, you may have difficulty feeling good about yourself, and so you are tempted to avoid any conflict that could cause more negative feelings. Silence becomes your defense. But you pay a price for not putting your feelings and views into words. The feelings that stay bottled up within you can cause all manner of mayhem, from headaches to anxiety to loneliness. You may also feel phony, knowing that you have not expressed yourself honestly and may have been perceived to hold views that are actually antithetical to your own. You envy the freedom of those who are outspoken, but your lack of confidence keeps you silent, tense, and frustrated.

A dearth of self-confidence or a sense of inferiority might silence you, but if silence is not your style, you might try to cover your uncertainty with exaggeration. You fear that simply stating a fact might reveal your feelings of inadequacy, so you embellish the truth. Alex came from a middle-class family yet manages to convey to new acquaintances how successful his father was by mentioning that it has been difficult to adjust to the size of his present home when the home he grew up in was so huge. Brenda grew up in a rural area where having a horse went along with having cows and chickens. But she narrates riding old Nellie as though she had put a $300,000 thoroughbred through her paces. Embellishing the facts to cover doubts of self-worth is a stressful endeavor, but many people habitually attempt it. Such talking not only causes others to mistrust you but also encourages you to be suspicious of others—not a productive way to create trusting relationships.

## Evading the Truth

Fibs and evasions share the field with exaggerations and embellishments. They are not serious lies. The speaker does not preplan them and does not intend to harm. Fibs are usually knee-jerk reactions to keep the speaker from appearing deficient. When Jack, who is heading up a project, turns to Sam and asks for the quarterly report, a report that totally slipped Sam's mind, Sam replies, "The numbers haven't come in yet. They should all be compiled by Monday." The possibility of Sam simply saying, "I forgot," is too painful to consider. So he fibs, like a three-year-old caught with a hand in the cookie jar and for nearly the same reason; he hopes that he sounds more convincing than the toddler. Evasions are more oblique than little white lies. Your spouse seems about to ask you if you paid the bills that are still sitting on your desk, so you adroitly switch the topic and ask, "By the way, when are we going to visit your mother? I think she expects to see us this summer." You don't want to admit the truth that you didn't pay the bills; you don't want to look bad. So you evade her disappointment—for the moment. Your evasions ultimately create an atmosphere of distrust and second-guessing.

## Speaking Impersonally

One way to seek "safety" interpersonally is to keep your feelings well separated from your intellect. If you are particularly bright, then avoiding feelings and focusing only on your thoughts, opinions, and insights can seem an unassailable manner of interacting. Emotions are messy, whereas the intellect seems clean and respectable. Sadly, the path of the intellect will lead to trouble when your relationships demand more of you. When your spouse insists that you share your feelings, you get exasperated, unable to share one emotion, let alone the myriad of others with which you are not remotely familiar. And you experience further frustration at work when coworkers evaluate you as cold and distant. Such experiences can seem distinctly unfair. Why must you have to deal with feelings? Why not simply be rational? The answer, even to your intellect, is simple. You are more than your brain, and more of you is wanted and needed by those who relate with you.

You might have formed habits that shield you by focusing your attention on others and on what you think might be good for them. If this describes you, you tend to begin your sentences with "you," not "I." You advise your friend, "*You* should stop smoking." "*You* are not eating enough." "*You* shouldn't talk to your son like that." Or you accuse your partner, "*You* always think of yourself." "*You've* never given me what I need." "*You* drink too much." Or you tell your children, "*You* are lazy." "*You* don't work as hard as your brother." "*You're* making too much noise." Reflecting on your candor, you congratulate yourself for "saying it like it is." But you haven't shared yourself. You haven't let your friend know you, as you would by saying, "I feel frightened when I see you smoking and not eating enough. I couldn't bear losing you." You allow your son to appreciate your needs by admitting, "I feel irritated and distracted when I'm writing and you have your music blaring." You might profit from reflecting on the words from scripture, "How dare you say to your brother, 'Let me take the splinter out of your eye,' when all the time there is a plank in your own" (Mt 7:4–5).

Transparency, telling the truth, being totally open, revealing yourself without qualification or fig leaf is, in Shakespeare's words, "a consummation devoutly to be wished." But in the real world, where love and understanding, compassion and trust are too often absent, total transparency remains more a wish than a fact. In its place, habits of indirect communication are born. Sometimes these behaviors are necessary and meet your needs. You have a right to be silent at times, and occasionally your friend profits from a piece of your advice. Sometimes you really need to ask a question or to make a judgment. When these behaviors become habits, however, they do not satisfy the need you have for greater intimacy, fuller expression, and trust from those with whom you work or live. Acknowledging your habits is a necessary first step to replacing them with more authentic and effective communication skills. Reflect on your own style of communicating as you read the following chapters, which discuss some frequently used indirect forms of expression.

## ■  FOR  REFLECTION  ■

1. Can you identify the ways in which you speak that do not reveal yourself in an authentic manner? When and with whom are you your most real self?

2. Can you describe the feelings that you have when you are reluctant to speak?

3. Are there times when you know you are talking too much? Do you know what you are feeling at these times?

4. When you realize that you are saying "you" when you mean "I," do you know what is going on inside of you that leads you to speak impersonally?

5. Can you remember an instance when you were judged? How did you feel?

# Chapter Seven

# speaking impersonally

Talking much about oneself may be a way of hiding oneself.

—Friedrich Nietzsche

## Putting Distance between Self and Self-Expression

"When you step onto the moon . . ." These were Neil Armstrong's opening words when asked in an interview about his lunar experience. *You?* Armstrong obviously didn't mean to imply that his interviewer had or could "step onto the moon." Since only a dozen humans out of 6.5 billion living on earth have indeed stepped onto the moon, the astronaut had to be talking about himself. So why didn't he say, "When *I* stepped onto the moon"? Maybe he was trying not to appear boastful as the first person to revel in the awesome experience of making footprints on the moon's surface, so he employed the inaccurate and impersonal pronoun "you." But we all understand. We automatically translate. The "you" means "I," and we listen to hear Armstrong describe *his* unique experience.

Joe Drape, a *New York Times* sports reporter, began his article about the 2009 Kentucky Derby, "Sometimes this game brings you to tears." A reader would be excused for thinking, "Not really. Doesn't bring me to tears. Personally, I hate the thought of these beautiful thousand pound animals risking their lives running on skinny little ankles." Drape continues to depict a stunning upset victory from unlikely sources: "A Cajun jockey and $9,500 gelding send tears streaming down your face." Most people root for an underdog, and their reactions to an upset victory may range from disbelief to delight to regret for not placing a bet. And, surely, they might be moved, even to tears. But is the reporter presuming all fans or spectators are reduced to tears? No, again the reader translates. It was Joe Drape who cried in response to the gelding Mine That Bird, a 50-1 long shot, winning the annual Run for the Roses. Well, if ol' Joe was so affected emotionally, why didn't he just say so? Maybe sports guys don't cry. Maybe he was admitting a lot already just to talk of crying; putting "I" with tears could have sounded too personal, a bit too revelatory. So he fudged a bit and said "you" when really he was talking about himself.

Saying "you" instead of "I" is so common that we don't have to learn to translate. It is sometimes the American equivalent of the French "on" and the English "one," as in, "One loves a strong cup of tea." The French and the English use an impersonal "one" to substitute for the personal "I." The Queen employs the royal "we" to serve the same purpose. "We were not amused" refers not to her subjects being displeased but to herself. Perhaps Americans find the English "one" stiff or pompous, and they have no pretensions to royalty. "You" serves as their acceptable substitute for "I." So when Armstrong uttered, "When you step onto the moon . . ." instead of objecting, "Are you kidding?" we know that he means himself. And when Drape writes that horseracing can "bring you to tears," even ones "streaming down your face," we understand that *he* was moved and he cried.

## Speaking Impersonally Avoids Exposure

All day long most of us habitually say "you" when we mean "I." But probably we are not aware that we are hiding ourselves by doing so. Saying "I" exposes the speaker. Saying "*I* feel sad when I pass a homeless person" makes us more visible and more vulnerable than saying, "*You* feel sad passing a homeless person." Admitting our own sadness at seeing someone lying in a doorway could persuade someone to see us as too soft or sentimental. Our admission could prompt someone to react, "Hey, man, get a grip. You'll wear yourself out feeling sorry for people you don't even know." It's safer to say, "*You* feel sad," than, "*I* feel sad." Since feeling safe from criticism or rejection always seems preferable to feeling vulnerable, we learn to say "you" repeatedly until it becomes our habitual way of talking.

We might also use the pronoun "you" instead of "I" as a tacit appeal for support. When we say, "You feel sad passing a homeless person," we could be hoping that the listener will chime in with a similar feeling in the same situation. It would be more accurate, then, to be saying something like, "I feel sad passing a homeless person. Don't you?" Whether we substitute "you" for "I" as a slight protection, as a plea for support, or just because we so frequently hear others use it, we develop the habit of using "you." Even when we are not thinking that we need protection, out pops "you," although we evidently mean "I."

A client said to us recently, "You just get so tired battling depression." Another said, "You blow up and then you wish to God you hadn't." The first client wasn't saying that his therapists were depressed, and he wasn't at all afraid to admit his depression. He was just used to saying "you" instead of "I." The same is true of the second person. She wasn't accusing her therapist of having an anger problem. Obviously it was her own that she was ruing. Yet she said "you." Saying "you" when "I" is the appropriate pronoun might seem harmless enough. We all do it, and we understand to whom the one speaking is referring. But there are consequences to this substitution of pronouns, the chief one being a lessening of personal contact. If you state, "You feel lonely when your friends are away," you are making yourself less personally present to your listener than if you own, "I feel lonely when my friends are away." You are even a little less present to yourself.

Say out loud an emotion that you have felt recently. First, use the pronoun "I": "I feel _____ (emotion)." For example, "*I* feel

excited seeing my new apartment." Then make the same statement using "you": "You feel _____ (emotion)." "*You* feel excited
seeing your new apartment." Did you feel the difference in the
experience of these two statements? You probably felt your
emotion run through you again when you said "I." Saying
"you" removed you verbally and emotionally from yourself.
When you put your feelings into sentences starting with "I,"
you *own* them as yours and experience them as you voice them.
Your words put you in touch with yourself, make you present to
yourself. That presence or connection to self is necessary if you
are going to be present, to connect emotionally, with someone
else. When you declare, "I feel more alive in the springtime,"
you reveal you to yourself and to someone else more than if you
said, "You feel more alive in springtime."

## Saying "I" Fosters Personal Interaction

When we use the word "I" to express ourselves, we are more
visible, and so we also encourage the person to whom we are
talking to be open. Our openness inspires openness, makes it all
right for the other to disclose. The result is personal connection.
Statements that begin with "you" tend to hide the speaker and
lead to an impersonal discussion. "I didn't know what to say to
Jane at Henry's wake" invites the listener to learn about you, to
come to know you. The listener can feel free to respond by sharing her own feelings, "I felt so tongue-tied myself. I just stood
next to her and hoped she'd feel my support." Saying "you"
triggers a very different reaction, one that is less personal. For
example, the remark, "You don't know what to say to someone
who has lost a spouse," may elicit an impersonal response such
as, "Well, you don't, do you? Grief is such an individual thing."
This comment could lead to a discussion of grief or the awkwardness of wakes. There is certainly nothing wrong with that
discussion. If the speaker wanted that type of conversation, then
saying the second statement might introduce various valuable
topics, such as the expression of sympathy, the privacy of grief,
or the purpose of wakes. But if the speaker wanted to share her
feelings of awkwardness and regret, then starting with "you"
could readily thwart her goal and start a discussion that might
be interesting but not what she was seeking.

To communicate in a way that satisfies your needs, you have to be aware of your purpose in talking. Are you attempting to relieve your feelings by expressing them? Are you trying to reveal yourself to a friend? Are you sharing personally to satisfy a need for understanding or support? Are you simply talking to make light conversation? Many interactions can drain your energy rather than energize you if you have not been alert to your needs and intentions.

If you want to chat impersonally, then using the impersonal "you" fits the bill. "You've got to love those Mets." "You never know where this market is going." Impersonal comments and conversation are essential aspects of human interaction. They demonstrate friendliness without inviting unwanted intimacy. They are an antidote to awkwardness and are the fodder for chitchat and small talk. So if your goal in talking is to be impersonal, use "you" to mean, you know, everyone.

> To communicate in a way that satisfies your needs, you have to be aware of your purpose in talking.

If your intention in talking, however, is to make yourself known, to reveal your feelings and needs, hopes and plans, then your words should do exactly that. Starting with the word "I" is direct and indispensable. When you say, "I feel," "I believe," "I think," you are revealing yourself, admitting what is happening in your life, in your heart, and in your mind. You are expressing your feelings and your experiences, so allow your words to do just that, to focus on yourself. Be personal; say "I."

■ FOR REFLECTION ■

1. Try to use the word "I" throughout the day. Ask yourself when and why saying "I" instead of "you" felt uncomfortable (or comfortable).

2. Do you know what you are feeling when you switch from "I" to "you"? Is the switch intentional?

3. When are you most likely to speak impersonally?

# Chapter Eight

# *asking questions*

Ask me no questions and I'll tell you no fibs.

—Oliver Goldsmith, *She Stoops to Conquer*

## Questions Obscure the Speaker's Intention

"So what's wrong with asking questions?" asked Nathan belligerently from the back row at a communications seminar we were conducting for the sales staff of a pharmaceutical company. As leaders of the program, we could have answered Nathan in a number of ways. Asking questions is a problem because:

■ questions can put the one being asked on the defensive;

■ behind every question lies a statement, and it would be more direct to make the statement;

■ questions tend to hide the feelings, needs, and opinions of the one asking while expecting the one being asked to reveal his or hers;

■ questions are not the most effective way to establish a trusting connection.

Or we could have answered, "There doesn't have to be anything wrong with questions. All of us need to ask questions to get directions, to solve problems, to acquire information. There are endless situations that propel us to pose appropriate questions." In short, we could have simply answered his question.

But to make real contact with Nathan—authentic, personal encounter being the focus of the seminar—Nathan would need to identify his feelings behind the question, and we would need to acknowledge these feelings before answering the question. Then the question becomes, does Nathan know his feelings and is he willing to reveal them? In the incident that we are describing, Nathan gradually was able to identify the feelings that prompted his question and to share them at our invitation: "I admit I felt irritated when you listed questions as a type of ineffective communication. I ask questions all the time. I don't see anything wrong with that." We listened to Nathan before answering. In doing so, we learned what Nathan was feeling. We were able, also, to acknowledge his desire to defend his practice of asking questions. As we listened, Nathan clarified for himself what lay behind his question. As he talked, he grew less irritated and more understanding, not only of himself, but also of the way that questions can be triggered by feelings while at the same time mask them. The interaction was satisfying for Nathan and for us. In answering the surface content of a question, we frequently miss the person making the inquiry. The individual often needs attentive listening to make clear to himself what he is really meaning to ask. Often, he realizes that he is actually making a statement that needs no answer at all.

> In answering the surface content of a question, we frequently miss the person making the inquiry.

Another example of the need to listen before answering the question involves our client Patrick. During his first session, Patrick had expressed gratification with the insights he was receiving from us. At one point, he had imitated the character played by Robert DeNiro in the movie *Analyze This*, saying, "You're good. You're good." His first words in the second session, however, were, "What are your credentials? Where did you go to school? Are you medical doctors?"

Instead of answering his questions, we explored with Patrick the reason behind them. He responded, "I hope you don't mind, but my wife wants to know." We delved further into Patrick's feelings about his wife's concerns. He burst out emotionally, "I felt resentful. It just shows how she doesn't respect me." Patrick went on to discuss his relationship with his wife and how he feels demeaned by her. He acknowledged further resentment at what he saw as her interference with his therapy.

Had we answered immediately with a summary of our education, training, and experience, Patrick would not have realized his feelings or the fact that he was bringing his wife's agenda into his counseling session. We would not have learned about our client. We had not been reluctant to talk about our education and experience but had wanted to ascertain the deeper concerns we were addressing. When we did offer to provide credentials, Patrick demonstrated polite interest and a desire to get on with *his* agenda for the session.

## Forms of Questions

Questions fall into three categories, each of which serves a purpose, yet also produces unforeseen consequences:

1. Rhetorical

2. Informational

3. Empathic

### Rhetorical Questions

A speaker does not intend for rhetorical questions to be answered. These questions are statements disguised as questions for effect. Shylock in Shakespeare's *The Merchant of Venice*, for example, is not really asking questions of his gentile audience when he says, "If you prick us, do we not bleed? If you tickle us, do we not laugh?" He is pleading with them to realize that Jews are as human as they are. Similarly, if a mother asks her thirteen-year-old daughter, who wants new sneakers, "Do you think money grows on trees?" mom does not want to hear,

"Of course not, Mom. You should know that money is printed by the US Mint, a department of the US Treasury." When Dad chimes in, "Do you think I'm made of money?" he wants chagrin from his daughter, not a biological report of the human body's composition. Rhetorical questions, not too subtly, veil the speaker's emotion—often irritation or exasperation—behind a question that tends to be tinged with sarcasm.

Rhetorical questions frequently provoke a resentful reaction. The insult entailed in the sarcasm doesn't augur well for respectful dialogue. Since rhetorical questions are not intended to prompt literal answers and since they often generate hard feelings, it might be productive to avoid them. If you are tempted to resort to a rhetorical question, try stating your feelings directly instead.

*Indirect*: Do you think money grows on trees?

*Direct*: I feel impatient that you are asking for new sneakers so soon after buying the ones you are wearing.

*Indirect*: Do you think I'm a mind reader?

*Direct*: I feel hurt when you don't tell me what you are thinking.

## Informational Questions

Daily life requires information. We all spend part of every day seeking answers to our questions. We "Google," "look it up," "check it out," or simply ask, "What time is it?" "Who won the game?" "When are we supposed to arrive?" These questions are usually resolved with simple answers. Even these harmless questions, though, conceal meaning behind them, but the questioner and the recipient of the question assume that the meaning is obvious, and all that is required is the answer. Fear of being late might be the motive for asking about the time, and an accurate telling of the time is all that is required. But other questions mask, by intention or not, a statement that needs to be addressed. Some of these questions we call "loaded questions." They're laden with implied threat, loaded as a gun ready to blast you for your answer:

- "When *were* you going to tell me about the check that bounced?"

- "What time *did* you leave the bar?"

- "Why did you say you had done *all* of your homework?"

Instead of threatening the listener with your "loaded question" and thereby prompting a defense that you don't want to hear, you could state your feeling directly:

- I am so frustrated, not just that you bounced a check, but that I felt so stupid when the auto shop called to complain.

- I don't trust you when you say you left the bar by eleven. I hate it when I think you are lying to me.

- I feel resentful. You had all weekend to do your homework and now you are going to stay up half the night to get it done.

Loaded questions are at least blatant—the questioner's feelings, though unstated, are easy to recognize. Many informational questions truly hide the one asking. These kinds of questions stir in the recipient a range of feelings from confusion and misunderstanding to defensiveness and hurt, hardly useful feelings in the person from whom you need an honest answer.

A wealthy, newly married couple was house-hunting in Newport, Rhode Island, dreaming of starting their new life together there. They had mentioned to the real estate broker a love of sailing. While viewing a home on the water on what was quite a blustery day, the wife asked, "Is it always so windy?" The broker, presuming wind is highly desirable to a sailor, assured her "Oh, yes, the wind is strong every day." The only thing the wife was assured of was that Newport was not for her. She disliked strong wind. The broker presumed that he had heard in the wife's question a statement of her desire for good sailing conditions. Like many presumptions to questions, his was wrong.

A college student shared the hurt and confusion that she feels in phone conversations with her father when he asks, "Have we covered all the bases?" She said to us,

I don't know what he means. I don't know if he wants to end the call or if I'm boring him. It makes me feel like he's conducting a business meeting. Maybe he doesn't mean anything at all or maybe he's uncomfortable. I'd really like to know why he asks that.

Informational questions might seem both innocuous and necessary, but the requests can be ineffective if the speaker uses them to make personal contact. This father's question bewilders his daughter when he might really be saying, "I'm loving talking with you, so is there anything else we can talk about?" or "I don't want to miss anything going on with you that's important to you. Anything else you want to share?"

Intimacy is impossible if there is not reciprocity in sharing.

Some people use questions as a way of starting conversations. From time to time this approach can be effective, but it can also tend to be one-sided. It invites the other person to talk, but it can keep the questioner hidden. A good friend of ours has a unique style of making new acquaintances. He's a gregarious person and takes genuine pleasure in meeting new people. He'll see someone he hasn't met before, note something special about the individual's dress or reading material, and ask a question such as, "I saw you reading *Gulliver's Travels*. Now, what made you pick up that old chestnut?" He makes an observation and then asks a question. He learns a lot about other people and enjoys telling their stories in conversation with others. It's notable, though, that he rarely shares anything about himself. He's a master at drawing others out with his intriguing questions while remaining the invisible man. The one emotion he does occasionally share is that he's lonely. Intimacy is impossible if there is not reciprocity in sharing. Our friend's perceptive questioning style is good for getting people talking but not for deepening a relationship. Many people love to talk if someone expresses an interest. Our friend becomes a willing sounding board. But he doesn't reveal his own feelings, concerns, or problems, and as a consequence is lonely.

Ed learned from the "mouths of babes" the ineffectiveness of questions to facilitate personal contact. Ed is a brilliant university professor with two adorable tots aged six and eight. He described his determination to become more personally involved in their lives and laughed as he recounted his futile attempts to engage them in conversation while picking them up from school. "I always ask, 'How was school?' My six-year-old says, 'Fine,' and pulls out a game." Ed burst out laughing when he reported, "My daughter pays so little attention to the question that she often doesn't answer at all." Ed was quick to realize that he was putting as little effort into his question as the children were into their answers. He recognized that, in order to elicit their responses, he needed to focus on giving them full attention. He learned to greet them in new ways; for instance, "I've missed you guys. I'm the luckiest dad in the world to have you two." Ed is learning to put his interest and his love into words that actually convey his desire to know them.

Ed has discovered that some questions can prompt his children to tell him about themselves. The most effective questions must reveal his knowledge of them and their worlds and must be very specific. "How was recess? Who did you play with? Who did you sit next to at lunch? What happened with your friend who was mad at you yesterday?" Ed has recognized that to ask questions that truly connect him to his son and daughter, he has to know their school schedules to be able to ask, "What are you doing in art class?" "What did you do in gym today?" He has become more sensitive to his son and daughter and more alert to when they need to be quiet and when they want to talk. Also, he has discovered new ways to be with them. Recently, he brought his daughter to one of his lectures and introduced her to his class. When the class applauded her, she beamed. "I think I asked the wrong question, though, as we walked to the car," he laughed ruefully. "I asked her what she thought of my lecture and she said, 'It was a little bit boring.' But she chatted all the way home."

### Empathic Questions

Loaded informational and rhetorical questions cannot adequately achieve trusting interaction. Empathic questions have more of a chance to reach that goal. These questions focus on the person you are talking to and on his or her feelings. In this way empathic questions differ from informational ones; they are questions asked not to meet your agenda—to gather information or to satisfy your curiosity—but to unite with the other by listening to his feelings, by empathy. Suppose your friend tells you that her brother lost his job.

> Informational question: What did he do?
>> Source of the question: Your curiosity
>> Focus of the question: Your friend's brother and his work
>
> Empathic question: Are you afraid he'll get depressed?
>> Source of the question: Care for your friend
>> Focus of the question: Your friend and his or her feelings

In another instance, your son tells you that a boy in his class was suspended for having marijuana in school.

> Informational question: How long is the suspension?
>> Source of the question: Your curiosity about the school's drug policy
>> Focus of the question: School rules
>
> Empathic question: Are you worried about him?
>> Source of the question: Care for your son
>> Focus of the question: Your son's feelings

Empathic questions convey care and interest to the person with whom you are talking. They help connect you with that person by directing your focus on him or her. You do not ask to satisfy your own curiosity about the content (job loss, school drug policy), but to connect you on an emotional level with another person. You are not using a question to make a point, or to gather data that you can use to give advice, or to blame or punish. You are asking an empathic question that attempts to understand the other person. Your intention is to provide the person with the opportunity to put his emotions into words. "Are you feeling discouraged that the trip was cancelled?" "Do you have stage fright before speaking?" So, with that intention, your empathic questions can achieve understanding and satisfying contact. If your timing is right and your interest trusted, the person asked might feel open to respond and grateful for the opportunity.

With questions, you risk asking the other person to reveal feelings while keeping yours unspoken. So if you ask an empathic question, be sure that your intention is a genuine desire to understand. You might want to make that intention clear in your words

> Remember, behind every question is a statement.

before asking, "I was concerned for you when I heard that your trip was cancelled. Did you feel discouraged when you couldn't go?" "I was very impressed by the relaxed way that you spoke. Do you ever feel stage fright?" Remember, behind every question is a statement. Try to be aware of yours when you start to ask a question. It might be more productive to state it openly.

■ F O R   R E F L E C T I O N ■

1. *Can you think of a time when you automatically answered a question and then regretted that you responded so quickly? What caused the regret?*

2. *Can you identify the kinds of situations in which you find yourself asking more questions than perhaps are necessary? Do you ask questions when you are nervous? When you are anxious? When you are skeptical?*

3. *Can you describe how you felt in a particular situation when you were the recipient of questions?*

# Chapter Nine

# *withholding yourself*

And if you care, don't let them know
Don't give yourself away.

—Joni Mitchell, "Both Sides Now"

I am not from a background where people talk about problems in their relationships. If someone does or says something that upsets you, you don't say so. Maybe it's another Presbyterian thing; if the Eleventh Commandment is Thou Shalt Not Emote, the Twelfth is Thou Shalt Not Admit To Being Upset, and when it becomes evident to the whole world that you are upset, Thou Shalt On No Account Explain Why. No, you swallow your feelings, force them down inside yourself, where they can feed and grow and swell and expand until you explode, unforgivably, to the utter bewilderment of whoever it was who upset you.

Kate Morrison describes herself and her background in these sad words. She is a character in a novel, *Crow Lake*, by Mary Lawson, but she could be speaking for any number of the clients we have counseled. These women and men learned not to talk in their families and, in order not to talk, they found it was easier not to feel. Awareness of feelings might have forced their expression and that wasn't allowed. So these individuals ignored, suppressed, and repressed the emotions, big and small, churning within them. They developed a habit of being silent. "Silence like a cancer grows," Simon and Garfunkel sing. Silence can be deadly to psychic health and isn't good for physical health either. We need to talk to be healthy. Silence can also be lethal to relationships. Kate, like many of our clients who were scarred by suppressive environments, complains that her boyfriend, Dan, asks more of her than she can give. Dan blames Kate for shutting him out of her life. To the person who has learned to be silent in order to be safe, being asked to talk feels like being pushed into dangerous and potentially painful territory. However, trying to connect deeply with the silent individual can be exasperating, like grasping at air.

One client described her lonely frustration with trying to grow closer to her spouse. "I told him, 'I share everything with you. I tell you my fears, my self-doubt. You never open up.' I said, 'You've got to have feelings like that too.' He said, 'I don't go there.' And that was that." Another person shared with us at a workshop, "I know I frustrate my girlfriend. I like that she talks a lot. She feels everything. I would like to make her happy, but I'm who I am. And I feel insufficient next to her." Intimate relationships are demanding. Needs are intense, involving powerful emotions. Differences of personality, style, values, and background complement each other, but they also can be cripplingly divisive. It is not easy for spouses when one always wants to socialize while the other relishes solitude, or when one wants to "buy now" and the partner wants to save. Managing the tensions that differences can produce requires continual airing of thoughts and emotions. Silence sabotages discussion and squelches understanding, rendering the resolution of conflicting views impossible.

## Family Influence

Backgrounds do not have to be stifling to instill a reluctance to share feelings, needs, reflections, and experiences. Families develop all types of cultures that impede healthy communication. In some households, differences of opinion become combative, teaching the less aggressive spouse or child to keep head and voice down. Highly competitive environments can effect similar caution. In some families, a parent's fury forbids free expression of feelings and colors any strong emotion with negative associations. One sibling's hysterics results in another's reticence.

Messages in the family that restrict open expression are often reinforced in the community. "Children should be seen and not heard," "Women don't get angry," "Big boys don't cry," "Be nice," "If you don't have anything nice to say, don't say anything at all" are blatant or subtle admonitions that discourage frank expression of feelings.

> Families develop all types of cultures that impede healthy communication.

Teachers, ministers, relatives, and neighbors, in a desire to maintain order or to impose their values, can contribute to a climate of repression. A highly creative woman who had suffered anxiety and depression traced these conditions to parental teachings that she be "ladylike" and quiet. She told us, "I felt furious when my father said that I should keep my daughter Shaundra quiet. I kept quiet when I was a little girl, and I love that my daughter speaks up." Another mother reported a similar reaction to a teacher's recommendation that her son learn to keep his mouth shut. "I cherish his boldness and confidence. He is respectful, but he speaks his mind."

## Silence for the Introvert and the Extrovert

Silence is destructive when it forbids free voicing of feelings and views. Yet, silence in itself is necessary for reflection, for solitude, for rest. Some individuals require more quiet than others. Introverted personality types, for example, before talking need extra time to process their experiences, to shape their thoughts, and to clarify their feelings. Extroverts can be puzzled by a spouse, child, or friend who needs quiet time more often than they do. The extrovert might frustrate the introverted spouse by seeming to act without first thinking through all the ramifications of his behavior. The extrovert, on the other hand, can feel that he needs the patience of Job to wait for his introverted spouse to take action. Since approximately 25 percent of the general population is introverted and 75 percent is extroverted, the introvert may feel odd being such a minority and may fear being seen as weird by her extroverted partner. The extrovert can be vulnerable to the thought that his spouse is viewing him as rash and superficial. They need to talk over and over, in situation after situation, to resolve differences and to unite harmoniously. Their differences can be complementary, producing a more dynamic and balanced relationship than if they were alike. Without discussion, however, their differences can prove divisive, pushing them apart.

## Punishing Silence

Silence is a destructive tool when it inhibits an individual from self-expression. It is equally destructive when it is employed intentionally to punish. A particularly harsh punishment inflicted on students in some English boys' schools was called "being sent to Coventry." The practice isolated the student from peer contact. No other student would speak to him. The effect was devastating. Many boys withdrew from school to escape this form of punishment, and some are known to have committed suicide. "Being sent to Coventry," however, is not isolated to English boarding schools. It is practiced in many homes and in many relationships. In his trilogy *The Norman Conquests*, Alan Ayckbourn masterfully displays the wickedness of penalizing silence. One character, Reg, remarks after a battle with his wife, Sarah, "Well, that should be good for a couple weeks of silence. She's good at that." The people in the audience laugh at Ayckbourn's characterization of punishing silence in married life because they are so uncomfortably familiar with the behavior.

"Freezing someone out was the weapon of choice in my family," a young man, Darren, remarked.

> Get this: if you said something to my father that he didn't like or something he didn't agree with, he would just stop talking in the middle of the conversation. He would literally close his mouth and walk away. Then a cold silence would settle over our house until he would decide that he wanted

to talk again. My mother just put up with it. No one ever asked him why he did that or why he eventually resumed talking. We just got used to it.

The problem with "getting used to it" was that Darren developed a similar way of dealing with disagreements—a behavioral pattern that steered him and his wife into marriage counseling. Without conscious thought, children imitate their parents' ways of showing or concealing emotions, particularly anger. They note the destructive, yet effective, outcome of someone's refusal to talk. They learn to tiptoe around the silent but apparently angry person so as not to incur his or her wrath. And at the same time, they fail to learn how to talk effectively through angry discord or how to bring about resolution. Withholding oneself, refusing to talk, so corrodes relationships possibly because it is the very opposite of love. Love gives of oneself through words and actions. It is "pure attention to the being of the other." Refusal to talk is blatant refusal to give attention. It is a refusal to love.

> Refusal to talk is blatant refusal to give attention. It is a refusal to love.

## Everyday Silence

We withhold ourselves, don't say what is going on within us, not only to punish; we keep quiet for all kinds of reasons. A woman who dreams of going back to school but doesn't share her dream with her husband says to herself, "There would be too many problems to solve: the kids, the money, the commute. Besides, he'd probably think it was silly." A fellow gets anxious that he might lose his job. He endures slight after slight from his boss, but he fails to confide in his wife. "She expects me to be strong. Why scare her?" A student keeps quiet in class when he would like to participate. He guards his silence, thinking, "I don't want to sound stupid." A patient doesn't ask for his blood test results even though he and his wife want to see them. He convinces himself silently, "The doctor will let me know if anything is wrong." Behind our silence and rationalizations for keeping quiet lurks fear: fear of being laughed at, fear of being rejected,

fear of being ignored. We keep quiet to avoid hurt, embarrassment, misunderstanding, or the threat of an argument. For some
people, failure to speak up can become a habit that they justify by
saying, "I'm just shy." No need to face the fears or to change. "I'm
just shy."

## The Harmful Effects of Withholding

We deprive ourselves and others by our silence. The woman
who dreams of returning to school isn't encouraged by her husband, who remains ignorant of his wife's longings. The man
who is demeaned by his boss suffers alone. His wife is kept distant, and even resented for her lack of support. Silence prevents
the quiet one from releasing pent-up feelings and giving voice
to his inner world. Silence, in addition,
keeps him from being known. He then
has difficulty trusting that he is fully
loved. As a client said, "I've always
feared that if I said out loud the things
I feel and think, no one would love
me." Many of us would concur with
this client's sentiment. We fear, "If you
only knew me," or, "Someday I'm
going to be found out." We think that
we are protecting ourselves by our
silence when in reality we are buttress-
ing our self-doubt. We fool ourselves into thinking that if we
remain somewhat hidden, we can control another's view of us.

> We fool ourselves
> into thinking
> that if we remain
> somewhat hidden,
> we can control
> another's view
> of us.

In reality, we reinforce our self-doubt by foregoing the experience of being liked or respected for exactly who we are. The
wife who doesn't share her dream of further education remains
fearful of her partner's judgment that she is silly. By sharing,
however, and then receiving his encouragement, she might dis-
pel her own doubts that she is foolish to think of herself as a student. Even if her partner were to disparage her plan, maybe she
could find the strength to assert herself, to appreciate herself,
and to see that his objections say more about him than they do
about her.

By our silence, we are doing a disservice to those who care for us. Not only do we cheat them of our presence, but we feed their own insecurities. When we are transparent, our friends, family members, spouse, child, and colleagues are able to see us accurately and to respond to our reality. When we are silent we become a *tabula rasa*, a blank slate, on which they will tend to project their own worst sense of themselves. Anita, an intelligent college student, described this phenomenon: "When my roommates don't talk to me, I'm sure that they think I am boring." She was reflective enough to add, "I'm probably the one who thinks I'm boring, but if someone doesn't talk to me, that's where I go." A mother spoke to us about her adult son: "When it looks as though he doesn't want to talk, I automatically conclude that he thinks I have been a poor mother." When the vice president of a large retail company was passed over for promotion, his wife called us to share her sadness. She was convinced that his withdrawn silence indicated his anger at her for not attending the company's previous Christmas party, an omission she had regretted guiltily for months. We tend to project our doubts about ourselves onto the person who is silent. If we see ourselves as fat or as not too brilliant or unstylish or unsuccessful, it doesn't take much silence for us to be convinced that that is exactly what the quiet person is thinking. Perhaps the awareness that your silence may be fodder for someone else's pain may encourage you to be more willing to open up. Your openness can help others ward off their own demons.

> When we are transparent, our friends, family members, spouse, child, and colleagues are able to see us accurately and to respond to our reality.

## Risks of Breaking Silence

In *The Courage to Be*, a profound treatise on the nature of courage, the theologian Paul Tillich writes, "The courage to be is the ethical act in which a man affirms his own being in spite of those elements of his existence which conflict with his essential self-affirmation." In all of us are elements that war with our need to accept ourselves, elements such as regret for our failings and awareness of our weaknesses and limitations. All the more, then, do we need courage to present our flawed selves openly and honestly to others. We realize as we make ourselves transparent that we are not invulnerable, nor immune to criticism. That is why the more that we have admitted and accepted our faults and foibles the more free we are to expose ourselves to the possible criticism, and even ridicule, of others. Our critic will not point to anything in us that we have not already confronted. John F. Kennedy wrote *Profiles in Courage*, keenly aware of the risks of speaking out in the face of potential harm. In his book, then-Senator Kennedy depicted the lives of eight senators who took bold, unpopular positions despite grave risk to their careers and vilification of their characters. The courage that we will require to speak up honestly will probably not be for great historical stands but for everyday moments:

- Expressing resentment to a colleague who has taken credit for your idea.

- Admitting hurt that your spouse failed to plan for your birthday.

- Confessing feelings of inferiority to a friend.

- Disclosing an embarrassing incident to a sibling.

- Owning up to a mistake or failure.

- Conveying admiration for another's achievement.

- Voicing delight in someone's participation or presence.

You risk when you share openly. You might be viewed as petty, insincere, or overly sensitive. Yet, nothing ventured, nothing gained. Brian Williams, the buttoned-down, smartly dressed anchor of *NBC Nightly News*, has begun to blog about his love of all kinds of music. He could have kept his passion to himself in the name of protecting his polished image. He didn't. He revealed himself and now he basks in the shared interest of thousands of music lovers. Withholding yourself checkmates possibilities for enriching interactions. So, as the Beatles sing,

"Let it out and let it in, hey Jude, begin." Begin to risk being more spontaneous and more giving—of yourself.

### ■ FOR REFLECTION ■

1. *Do you recall your original family's environment regarding speaking out and speaking up about feelings? Was your mother open? How about your father?*

2. *In your role in your family, were (are) you expected to speak or be quiet?*

3. *After an argument with a family member are you willing to talk things through? What makes you reluctant or willing?*

4. *What do you think to yourself that inhibits you from speaking? For example, do you find yourself thinking, "They won't understand," "They don't care," "It's irrelevant," "I'll sound like a whiner"?*

# Chapter Ten

# *fibbing and exaggerating*

He who permits himself to tell a lie once, finds
it much easier to do it a second and third time,
till at length it becomes habitual; he tells lies
without attending to it, and truths without the
world's believing him.

—Thomas Jefferson, "Letter to Peter Carr"

We talk to connect with others. The essential element of satisfying, effective human connection is trust. We give the accurate time to a couple who asks. They take us at our word and are able to get to their meeting on time. As social beings we need to trust that people talking to us regarding the time, the proper direction, the outcome of a game, or the result of a study are telling the truth. We rely on others to be honest when talking about an event or about themselves. Trust is a social bond essential to communal living. It calls on us to be men and women of our word and invites others to be confident in trusting our word. In the most intimate relationships, our happiness rests on a trusting

> The essential element of satisfying, effective human connection is trust.

response to our partners, family members, and friends when they say, "I love you." Interaction between people relies on the assumption or the hope that the words being spoken are true. Frequently, however, all of us for various reasons at various times betray that trust.

Christopher Buckley, son of author William Buckley, remembers the first time he heard his socialite mother lie:

> So one night, when I was six or so, sitting with the grownups at the dinner table, I heard Mum announce that the "king and queen always stayed with us when they were in Vancouver." By the "king and queen," she meant the parents of the current queen of England. My little antennae went *twing*? I'd never heard my grandparents refer to a royal visit, which is a pretty big deal. I looked at Mum and realized— *twang!*—that she was telling an untruth. A big untruth. And I remember thinking in that instant how thrilling and grown-up it must be to say something so completely untrue—as opposed to the little amateur fibs I was already practiced at, horrid little apprentice sinner that I was, like the ones about how you'd already said your prayers or washed under the fingernails. Yes, I was impressed. This was my introduction to a lifetime of mendacity. I, too, must learn to say these gorgeous untruths. Imaginary kings and queens will be my houseguests when I am older!

Why would this socially prominent woman, married to one of America's most famous men, lie? Her son hints at the reason: "She grew up a debutante in a grand house in Vancouver, British Columbia—grand but Vancouver-grand, which is to say provincial." Pat Buckley didn't seem to feel that just being Pat Buckley from Vancouver was prestigious enough for the rarified air of New York high society, so she lied and felt more assured of fitting in by aligning herself with the royal family.

Why do any of us lie, fib, prevaricate, and exaggerate? Why don't we simply say it like it is? Few of us are serious liars; that is, we are not pathologically mendacious. Those who are, lie persistently in all types of situations, seemingly unprovoked and for no apparent reason. They are often removed from reality and are unable to differentiate between telling the truth and lying.

Psychologists theorize that the underlying cause of their mendacity is a deep-seated self-dislike often coupled with unconscious anger.

## Lying to Get Something

The rest of us know when we are not being truthful, and we have a pretty good idea why. We want something that we fear we might not get unless we lie. We fudge the truth to make ourselves look better. We withhold the truth to avoid a reaction that we dread, such as rejection, scorn, or criticism. We have many needs, and sometimes we think that a candid expression of the facts might not get our needs met. Teenage Rick wants to go out. His parents want to confirm that his homework is finished before granting permission. The truth could sentence Rick to his room so he lies, "Yes, it's all done." And he adds, to make his answer more credible, "We didn't have much anyway," or, "I got it done in class." Rick's father wants a new rifle. His wife asks, "Can we afford it?" Despite the fact that money is actually very tight, he responds, "Yeah, no problem. We're doing fine." Rick's mother wants to fit in at her book club so she reports that she enjoyed the selection the group had just completed. She actually hasn't even read it, let alone enjoyed it. Each member of this family wanted something. Each of them thought that lying was necessary to get it. On the spur of the moment, each of these individuals abandoned honesty in pursuit of their goal.

What kept Rick from saying, "I still have some history to read. It will take half an hour. Would it be okay if I did it later?" Why didn't Dad say, "I think that I can sell my old one. The dealer has a great sale on that I don't want to miss"? Mom could have said, "I actually didn't get a chance to read it, but I look forward to hearing what everybody thinks." They could have told the truth. But they instinctively feared that honesty would not be the best policy; it would be a risk and one that would rely too much on the leniency or understanding of others. Better not take a chance, they, consciously or unconsciously, concluded.

We are all tempted to lie if it appears that telling the truth could jeopardize what we want. We might lie about our age to be served a drink, about our experience to get a job, about our health to obtain insurance, about our income to get a mortgage. Some of these untruths we justify as necessary to deal with rules and restrictions that we think are unfair or unnecessary, but our lies can produce unwanted consequences.

> We are all tempted to lie if it appears that telling the truth could jeopardize what we want.

Chuck, an energetic father of three young children, had just arrived with his wife, Caitlin, at a dinner party hosted by friends. The baby had been crying when they left their house, so shortly after arriving his wife asked him to call the babysitter to confirm that all was well. He went outside to get a signal for his cell phone and dialed. No one answered. He tried again; still the babysitter did not pick up. He presumed that there was no problem or she would have called. Afraid, however, that his wife, who is very attentive to their children, would worry and even ruin the evening by wanting to return home, he told her, "Everything is fine. All the kids are asleep." They enjoyed the party and only when they got into the car to return home did he tell her the truth. Caitlin was livid and declared, "I can't trust you." Generally, Chuck acts with integrity, but in this instance he lied to protect his evening out and paid a severe price in the loss of trust from the person in his life he most respects. Chuck wanted to enjoy an evening out with his wife among friends. What he wants even more, though, is Caitlin's respect and trust. Like many of us, Chuck lied because he wanted something. Like Chuck, we often lose something more valuable than what our lie gains. Sometimes what we lose is respect for ourselves; sometimes it is respect from others.

## Lying to Be Someone

The Irish novelist and playwright Sebastian Barry tells the tale of Annie Dunne. Annie is a fifty-nine-year-old woman whose childhood bout with polio has left her with a humped back and a desperate yearning to be desired as "normal" girls are, girls like her sisters Dolly and Maud. She recalls the incident that started the web of a lie that she continued to weave.

I don't know what the truth is. One day on the big yellow stones of the dock I was walking and a sailor leaned out from his dirty cargo ship and asked me for a kiss. I did not even answer him, but passed on without a glance. Or maybe this memory was at first made up; at this distance I no longer know rightly. When I got back to our quarters in the castle I told Maud something of the kind, and embellished the story, I am sure, in telling. Because I did not want her to be thinking it was always Dolly and her that got the interest, and there might be a man in the end who might overlook my damnable hump and take a risk of loving me. Then that shadowy man became my sailor, and Maud often told her friends of my sailor, maybe even to bolster herself as well as me against this crookedy back. Till I came to believe in him myself, and lived many a year waiting for him, and am maybe waiting for him still, even though he was a queer little dark man on a Portuguese tramp steamer amusing himself by saying hello to a humpety girl on an idle Dublin Sunday—unless that is all invented, too.

Annie invented a lover because she wanted to be seen as lovable. Pat Buckley lied to be seen as from a family that hobnobbed with kings and queens. An Irish farmer and a New York socialite were alike in not feeling sufficiently good enough about themselves. So they bolstered their image with a lie. We all want to be loved, liked, respected, and seen, if not better than others, then at least not worse. Many of us have difficulty believing that as we are we warrant esteem from others. We have trouble believing in our essential worth and trusting that "what you see" is sufficient. We know, often painfully, our weaknesses and our family's secrets. Other people can appear more popular, wealthier, better educated, or more athletic. So we tell lies or we shade the truth to look better than we see ourselves to be, fearing the way others may see us.

## Knee-Jerk Fibs

Sometimes our fibs are knee-jerk reactions offered to protect us from criticism. In reaction to the question, "Did you remember our anniversary?" we say, "Of course I did." When confronted with, "I thought you were going to pick up the dry cleaning," we quickly ad lib, "I stopped there but they had closed. I'll get it tomorrow." We fudge when asked, "Have you done the taxes?" "Yeah, I just need to put in a couple of receipts." We feel a bit guilty and maybe later wish that we had admitted the truth. We thought that the situation called for one quick lie to protect us, but often it requires additional lies and evasions that cause us more guilt and tension and may seriously arouse distrust in others—"Oh the tangled web we weave, when first we practice to deceive."

> So we tell lies or we shade the truth to look better than we see ourselves to be, fearing the way others may see us.

Knee-jerk fibs are triggered also when a reputation or image is threatened. If we are known as a movie buff, yet answer, "James Caan," when someone asks at a party, "Who was the actor in *Midnight Cowboy* with Dustin Hoffman?" we then spend the evening with the uneasy feeling that we were wrong. "Maybe it was John Voight." Perhaps the individuals at dinner know that we are in finance, so when the subject of derivatives comes up and all eyes turn to us we render an account that we hope sounds plausible, though we know that we are winging it with a vague notion of the facts. However, when we provide inaccurate data under perceived threat to the way that we are seen, we mislead and even baffle others, sometimes prompting them to wonder if we really know what we are talking about.

## Exaggerating

Tom complains, "I haven't slept for a week." Dick boasts, "I never forget a face." Harry says, "I'm just not eating." Not true, really. Tom has had one bad night's sleep, not seven. Dick remembers some faces, not all. Harry's appetite has waned, but he's not starving. Because the facts may not have the desired impact, the speakers embellish them. We joke of the fish that gets bigger with each telling. Granddad's hike to school when he was a boy gets longer as the years go by. The hot summer that

Mom remembers in her first year of marriage has more and more days above a hundred degrees. And Aunt Beth hasn't enjoyed many of the classics; she has read "all of them." Maybe the reason Pinocchio's nose grows when he lies is that many lies do too—they are often stories that, like the puppet's nose, grow with the telling. Hyperboles might seem innocent enough, but they can infiltrate the way that we talk with the result that, as we attempt to make ourselves a little smarter, our accomplishments somewhat grander, and our pain a bit more intense, we make ourselves a little less trustworthy.

We can be uneasy even when we state facts if we realize that these facts might seem misleading. Maybe that is why we are uncomfortable drafting a résumé, since it requires us to list experiences and accomplishments. We know that the summer in Biarritz was spent more in cafés than in classrooms, but we include it. And that project enrolling voters sounds impressive, but we know it was a fiasco. We feel queasy misleading. Most of us want to be transparent and desire to tell the truth.

When a friend or colleague is talking, we want to accept him at his word. We don't want the distraction of filtering his remarks through a mental fact-check. Others want the same from us. When we speak truthfully, others are free to accept what we are saying without being bewildered by inaccuracies or tricked by manipulation. Being honest, we earn their respect as well as their trust. Pressures of all kinds within us and in society lead us to fudge, fib, exaggerate, and even lie. Our ideals of honesty humble us yet also challenge and inspire. "Honest Abe" and George Washington who "couldn't tell a lie"—icons of integrity—beckon us to fib and exaggerate less and to risk more often by simply telling the truth.

■ FOR REFLECTION ■

1. Recall a time when you spoke about an event or an achievement in a way that was exaggerated or untrue.

2. What do you think prompted you to mislead your listeners?

3.  *In general, what feelings drive you to fudge the truth when talking about yourself?*

4.  *Do you avoid confrontation by speaking half-truths?*

# Chapter Eleven

# *judging*

Judge not lest ye be judged.

—Matthew 7:1

## Judgment vs. Transparency

Transparency is opening yourself, revealing who you are, and communicating who you are. In being transparent, you tell another person the truth about yourself. Judging is just the opposite. When you judge, instead of telling someone about you, you talk about him or her. Instead of giving yourself—your feelings, thoughts, needs, and dreams—you label others, telling them who they are. Suppose, for example, you and a friend are trying to complete a project. You have hit a snag due to conflicting ideas about how to proceed. You are frustrated but decide to say something, trusting that talking will resolve the logjam. "We have to get this done by the end of the week. You've got to stop being so stubborn and start being willing to consider other options." Your expectation that candor is necessary to

> Transparency is opening yourself, revealing who you are, and communicating who you are.

resolve conflict is well-founded, but in this case calling your friend "stubborn" probably causes her to react by arguing with you and defending herself. You haven't been candid; you've been judgmental and as a result intensified the conflict.

If you wanted to speak openly without judgment in an effort to resolve differences with your friend, you might say something like this: "I'm frustrated that we can't get past this one point, and I can't think of any options. I'm worried that you seem so convinced that this is the way to go that you, too, won't be able to come up with a new idea." *Your* concern, *your* worry, and *your* perceptions of her are now known. This time you have admitted your feelings rather than judged your friend. Your focus has been to share yourself, not to criticize or to judge her.

Honest sharing of yourself makes you vulnerable; judging makes the other person vulnerable. Transparency admits what is happening within you; judgment doesn't. When you judge, you focus on the other and identify who or, more accurately, what the other is: stubborn or soft, conceited or modest, rude or polite, hardworking or lazy, pretty or plain. For instance, imagine your sister has promised to call when she arrives home after a long drive in the pouring rain. When she still hasn't called several hours later, you call her and say, "Why didn't you call? You're so inconsiderate." You can become convinced that your judgment is valid and accurate, that it correctly characterizes your sister. Judging implies that you can evaluate the other person—in this case your sister—and that she doesn't know herself. It implies that you are right and the other is ignorant, uncaring, or just plain wrong.

None of us want to be judged. We know that even if we are considered to be a good person, we have many faults. We know that others' judgments miss so much of who we are that at best they are imprecise and often they are crushingly hurtful. We yearn to be known as we long to be loved. Most of us strive to understand ourselves, our conflicting motives, our choices that battle with our ideals, our needs that we often fail to meet, and our ambitions that we can't seem to satisfy. One day we are confident, another timid. We trust ourselves yet doubt ourselves. Like the great theologian Dietrich Bonhoeffer, we ask, "Who am I?" and then someone tells us; someone who thinks he knows, judges us.

He disregards our unique mystery and brands us: "You are bad," "You are selfish," "You are useless," even, "You are sweet." We don't want to be summed up in a judgment. But in our vulnerability and self-doubt, the judgment often sticks and is allowed to define us. That is why judgments are harmful and particularly dangerous to stamp on the young. We know judgments don't really capture who we are, yet we insist on our right and need to judge others. Indeed, there are many reasons that necessitate and justify judging; so, before demonstrating the harmful consequences of much judging, we'll outline some of the reasons our minds turn so easily to this behavior.

## The Need to Judge and Clarify

In trying to understand the world around us, we humans are confronted with an overwhelming variety of phenomena. Our minds, in an effort to make sense of this data, seek to organize it, as did our ancestors. Our ancestors grouped like things together. Some large growing objects they identified as trees, and put them in a separate category from others, which they labeled bushes. They saw differences between trees and defined them as evergreen or deciduous. Then they categorized the evergreens into specific types such as fir and spruce. In like manner, they divided the deciduous into oak, maple, elm, and so forth.

> We know judgments don't really capture who we are, yet we insist on our right and need to judge others.

They made distinctions between rocks, animals, and flowers. Like us they sought to understand by classifying and labeling.

Our minds need to name things to grasp their significance and meaning. Cognitive psychologists assert that we classify information to sort out our thoughts for decision-making. We need to organize our ideas into discrete thoughts to form concepts. And memory is enhanced by the economy of categories. In fact, as author George Lakoff writes, "Without the ability to categorize, we could not function at all, either in the physical world or in our social and intellectual lives." We humans are conditioned since antiquity to ask, what is it? Who is it? Is it animal, vegetable, or mineral? Friend or foe? In other words, we are conditioned to judge.

## The Need to Judge to Make Choices

Every day, dozens of times a day, we make choices, and choice implies judgment. We choose a Coca-Cola over a Pepsi or a Bud over a Miller because we judge one more pleasurable, tastier, lighter, or heavier than the other. We judge a carrot healthier than a cookie, applesauce as boring, and chocolate cake as decadent. Our choice is dependent on our judgment. Sometimes we have to modify our judgment to justify our choice. We select applesauce for dessert by amending our judgment from "boring" to "nutritious."

Our human family has been formed by choices, by what Darwin called "natural selection." Whether he was aware of it or not, our ancestral granddad was choosing grandma because he judged her as optimal for bearing his children, while grandma judged him as most capable of putting meat on the table. From earliest times humans have been selecting by judging. We judge when we buy a house, promote an associate, and select a movie. We judge the house to be overpriced or affordable, attractive or ghastly, colonial or contemporary, spacious or cramped. In hiring, firing, or promoting, we judge an individual as capable or incompetent, creative or conformist, a team player or showboat, smart or dull. In selecting a movie, we want to know if it is romantic, realistic, funny, or violent. We have to choose to live comfortably, and to choose we have to judge. So, if judging is ingrained in us and necessary for us to function, what is wrong with it?

## So What Is Wrong with Judging?

In personal relationships, judgments are usually unproductive and even harmful primarily because the one judging is usually unaware or unwilling to acknowledge the feelings that prompt his judgment. The judge considers himself as simply defining the one he is judging with the kind of objective detachment utilized when identifying a type of auto: "It's a Ford"; "He is incompetent." The one judging might say, "I have no feeling labeling this car a Ford; I am simply stating what it is." It is the same with judging the incompetent individual: "I am simply identifying that he is incompetent."

In fact, the one who's judging does have feelings regarding this person, and these feelings are often connected to needs that this particular individual is not meeting. We'll call the one who is quick to judge a manager, Jennifer, and the one being judged her employee, Elliot. If Jennifer needs Elliot to perform specific tasks, complete assigned projects, write up certain reports, and he doesn't fulfill these requirements, Jennifer could feel frustrated or impatient. She might worry that her own boss will be dissatisfied or fear that her department's quotas will not be reached. She could feel vulnerable to perceptions of herself as a poor manager or as a low producer. She could be angry that Elliot was "foisted" on her from another division of the company. She could have any number of feelings based on an array of needs. If she writes Elliot off as incompetent, she doesn't have to confront these dimensions within herself. In not acknowledging her feelings and needs, she has nothing to share with Elliott except calling him "incompetent." She probably resists being so blatant and therefore says nothing.

Jennifer doesn't weigh the option of sharing with Elliot the pressures she's under, the needs that she has to meet quotas, and/or her feelings of concern, frustration, or impatience. She is too focused on judging Elliot to reflect on her own needs and feelings, let alone the possibility of communicating them to him. She doesn't learn anything about herself or about him. Likewise, he doesn't learn from her or about her or about himself. Such judging blocks self-awareness, stifles effective interaction, and hinders any kind of learning.

Dorothea is an attractive, soft-spoken woman. She told us tearfully that she was desperate in her marriage. Her husband, Kyle, had been out of work for six months and according to Dorothea's description was not actively looking for work. "At first I thought he was not ambitious, then I thought maybe he was afraid to look for a job. Now I think he's just lazy." When we asked what she was saying to Kyle, she recoiled, "Oh my God. If

We hold onto our judgments at great cost to our own growth and to the development of our relationships.

I tell him he's lazy, he'll explode." Her judgments of Kyle were preventing her from speaking to him. Since she had not reflected on her own need that Kyle seek employment and on the emotions she had about his failure to do so, all she could think of saying to him was that he was lazy. In counseling she began to identify her feelings: concern for her husband, fear of losing their home, frustration at his lack of activity. We role-played how she would break the silence and risk sharing these feelings with Kyle. She reported back to us:

> We've begun, thank God, to talk. I understand him better and at least I feel like I'm not going to explode. I had no idea that he was hurting so much. He's almost paralyzed. His dad had been fired from an oil company and never worked again. Kyle's so scared he'll be like his dad. I feel closer to him now and together we'll get through this.

Dorothea learned that labeling her husband "lazy" blinded her to her own feelings and prevented her from comprehending the complex dimensions of her husband. By getting beneath her judgment of her husband, Dorothea was able to enrich their relationship. Her judgment of him became irrelevant and was replaced by understanding. Jennifer the manager had no such breakthrough. Her judgment defined Elliot once and for all; therefore, there was nothing to learn, and no room to grow. We hold onto our judgments at great cost to our own growth and to the development of our relationships.

Not only do feelings underlie judgments; if they are not admitted and expressed, feelings eventually produce judgments. When a friend hurts you and you don't acknowledge your feelings, that hurt will harden into a judgment of your friend: she's "insensitive." If you are angry with her, that unexplored or unexpressed anger may lead you to judge her, perhaps as "narcissistic." Your disappointment can become a judgment: "selfish." Your impatience can convince you that she's "stupid." And your gratitude can convince you that she is "generous."

All of us like to be right; once we have judged someone, we look at that person through the lens of our judgment in a way that validates our label. Judge your boss as pretentious, and her observations of the weather can sound pompous and her comments at the meeting can be clear evidence of her egotism. If you consider that boss brilliant, you could hear her weather remark as a sign of her perceptiveness and her words at the meeting as proof of her brainpower. We reinforce our judgments by gathering data that supports them while tending to ignore any evidence that might call our judgments into question. We duly note the boss's terse answer to a question, while we distrust her statement of apology.

> We reinforce our judgments by gathering data that supports them while tending to ignore any evidence that might call our judgments into question.

Another potentially destructive way that we bolster our judgments is by sharing them with others. We are careful to divulge our judgment with someone who won't challenge or contradict it. We tell an embittered colleague that our boss is insufferable as we provide a juicy tidbit of "evidence." We would never admit our negative judgment to the boss's loyal and enduring assistant. Our effort to reinforce our judgments by sharing them with others is especially harmful in undermining harmony among friends or in a family, group, or corporate setting. Judgments hamper, if not destroy, teamwork. When we judge, we limit our own ability to see another clearly; when we voice that judgment behind someone's back, we make it more difficult for others to give the person a fair chance of being known.

## Judging Hinders Knowing

When we judge, we categorize: this tree is an oak like all others of its kind, this car is a Ford like other Fords, and this man is skilled like all others we call skillful. This behavior is good for classifying members of groups, but bad for knowing the individual. The tree might be an oak like all oaks; but it is not like all oaks to the young woman who looks out on it from her window in all the seasons, who climbed it as a little girl, who lies under it to rest in its shade and look up into its awesome architecture of branches. It is not just any oak; it is hers. The Ford, too, is just a Ford to the categorizer, but to Jim it is his home on the road. In the Ford, he listens to music, has a place for his coffee, and even shaves. He knows its rattles and is aware when it is getting overheated. He has driven it to ease his loneliness and sped in it to blow out his anger. It's his baby. And this man is not just one of a group of skillful people; he is more than that. He is special to his wife. She trusts his know-how, relaxes when he puts his mind to fixing the washer, and delights in seeing him instruct their son in carpentry. To her, he is like no one else.

When we judge, we stand outside a person and label him. Judging simplistically sums up what he is: male, Irish, American, middle-aged, intelligent, relatively good-looking, successful, a good chap. To truly know the individual requires getting closer, learning to listen and appreciate the special qualities, traits, and abilities that make him unique. The only genuine label for this person is his name since it refers to his complete identity. Coming to know him is a never-ending process that involves listening to his thoughts, hopes, values, dreams, and convictions. And for him to trust you in a way that allows him to reveal himself to you, he will need to experience you as open to him, too. He will need to see you and know you as you wish to know him. Openness invites openness, or as Sidney Jourard, the author of *The Transparent Self*, writes, "Disclosure begets disclosure." Martin Buber refers to this trusting interaction when he writes, "All real living is meeting."

So is all learning. We don't really learn to understand anything or anyone from the outside. We have to meet them. We have to open ourselves—heart and mind—to experience a painting, a garden, our motorcycle, our dog, or our friend. We don't come to know a unique, one-of-a-kind individual, which we all are, by judging. In fact, by judging we fool ourselves into thinking we really do know a person. We've got him pegged. "He's a Democrat. What can you expect?" "She's a feminist; no sense bringing up the topic of maternity leave." We think that not only do we know someone, but we can predict his or her values, beliefs, and behaviors. Knowing the unique person requires that we be wary of our judgments and approach the other person with a willingness to listen and to learn. Knowing another person is demanding.

Judging, on the other hand, is easy—limiting, but easy. This behavior comes too readily. When as consultants we conduct a seminar on communication, we invite the participants to admit to themselves the judgments that they have made of everyone around the table or of many in the audience. Participants are sometimes painfully abashed that they have judged others so readily.

Really knowing someone is not easy. Maybe that is why such knowledge is absent in relationships of all kinds. Knowing someone requires that we know ourselves—our feelings, biases, needs, and perceptions. It demands honest sharing of ourselves and patient attention to another. Knowing the other is a process of revelation and discovery that happens as we meet that person openly. Judging isn't sufficient.

■ F O R   R E F L E C T I O N ■

1. *How would you define being transparent?*

2. *Think of a judgment you have made about an individual. How do you think your judgment affects the way that you relate with that person?*

3. *Think of a judgment that was made of you. How did you feel hearing this judgment?*

# Chapter Twelve

# *blaming*

The best years of life are the ones in which you decide your problems are your own. You don't blame them on your mother, the ecology, or the president. You realize that you are in control of your own destiny.

—Albert Ellis

Previous chapters have described attempts at communication that direct the speaker's attention away from sharing herself, and instead toward focusing on the other. Questions ask about other people. Judgments tell them who or what they are. A third kind of attempt at communication—blaming—follows this other-oriented pattern but in a more aggressive manner. Blaming tells the other that he or she is wrong and, not only that, but is also responsible for your dissatisfaction or hurt. You are innocent; the other is guilty. You are not responsible; he or she is.

When God asked Adam, "Have you been eating the fruit that I forbade you to eat?" our prime ancestor didn't hesitate: "It was the woman you gave to be with me, she gave me from the tree" (Gn 3:12). Husbands forever after have pointed the accusing finger at their wives. Wives are just as good at this blame game: "You did it (whatever *it* is), not me." Brother blames sister; sister cries, "It wasn't me. It's his fault." Students blame the teacher: "He gave me a D. He's so lame. He can't explain things." Teachers fault the students: "They pay no attention, don't study, and then expect an A." After a poor round, golfers denounce the greens as "too fast, too bumpy, and poorly maintained." After a day of not catching fish, the angler blames his companions: "They talk too much," or the water was "too rough," or his equipment was "lousy."

Effective communication requires that you acknowledge what is happening within you. To be understood, you have to express what you are thinking or feeling, observing or doing. In being honest you are taking responsibility for your emotions and reflections and actions. Blaming takes no such responsibility. When you blame, you don't focus on yourself; you focus on someone else. You forfeit the chance to be known, because you are not revealing yourself. If behind the blame you feel hurt or angry or sad, you have little chance of sharing these feelings. Your accusations probably put the persons you are addressing on the defensive, so that their energy is spent not in trying to understand you but on defending themselves. Blaming doesn't connect you with another person; rather, it drives the person away from you. It doesn't foster understanding or trust. Adam certainly couldn't have endeared himself to Eve with his spineless blame of her. Your blame of your spouse, child, friend, relative, or colleague can have no better chance of fostering a close relationship.

## Blame and Self-Justification

We blame others to protect our own egos. Self-esteem is everyone's quest and, for most men and women, an elusive goal. Compliments, praise, recognition, and accomplishments help to instill confidence and self-respect. But many of us need these affirmations like we need daily bread, provided over and over.

We have difficulty internalizing these positive endorsements in a way that makes us less dependent on them. Criticism, however, we absorb even as we experience it as a threat to our sense of self. We have enough trouble believing that we are good parents without hearing another parent say something about our son's "recklessness." Despite our self-doubts, we pride ourselves on our ability until our boss faults us for a project's failure. Comments that tell us that we are not as good, as smart, or as capable as we hoped to be are alarming. So we deflect the threat to our self-image by blaming someone else. "Johnny is not reckless. It's his friends who egg him on." "The project would have been done if the suppliers had come through on time." The golfer and the fisherman, too, feel threatened in their image of themselves so they blame whomever and whatever they can.

A key to stopping unproductive blaming is to start feeling better about yourself. Growth in self-esteem requires you to acknowledge your faults and limitations, to face up to what the psychologist Carl Jung called our "shadow side." You are not as vulnerable to someone pointing at a weakness in you if you have already admitted the weakness and done your best to combat or accept it. When you know and appreciate yourself, you are more able to accept criticism and take responsibility for your actions. You are then less prone to fault others. The ability to receive criticism enables you to change. Blaming others short-circuits your journey towards self-knowledge and self-esteem.

## Blame and Responsibility

"You make me angry." This statement sounds at first like you are attempting to share your feelings. In fact, you are blaming the other for your feeling. It is his fault that you are angry. "You make me sad." "You made me do it." These blaming comments all say, "I'm not responsible; you are." Being honest means taking responsibility for yourself, your feelings, and your reactions. Certainly your feelings respond to another's behavior, but they are *your* feelings; *you* are responsible for them.

Suppose, for example, your partner arrives home much later than usual. Your response might be to feel resentful. You could blame: "You make me so resentful." In other words, "It is your fault that I am resentful." In fact you feel resentful because of *your* perception of your partner's tardiness as well as *your* expectation that your partner would arrive earlier. If you read his lateness as a result of horrible traffic, you might feel compassion. If you interpret it as inconsiderate, you could feel resentful or hurt. It is *your* perception or interpretation that sets off *your* feelings. Plus, it is *your* expectation that he arrive earlier, maybe *your* need because you had a meal prepared or had plans that required him to be home. You have every right to your feelings, needs, and expectations. But they are yours and you have to take responsibility for them. Maybe you could have communicated your expectation earlier in the day, maybe you could have rearranged your plans, and maybe you might even need to lighten up about times and schedules. All that, *you* could examine. And you could still share honestly, "I felt resentful that you came home later than I expected. It seemed to me that you didn't care enough to call." *Your* feeling, *your* expectation, *your* interpretation—*your*self.

Your partner might hear blame and might defend or blame back. If you keep being responsible, maybe you could try to understand his reaction and then clarify that you are trying to tell him what it was like for *you* when he had not arrived; you are not telling him that he is bad. Communicating effectively means that you take responsibility for you, for your feelings, and for your intention in sharing at all.

## Blame Prompts Blame

Patti glared across the table in our consulting room at her husband, Scott, and spat out, "You don't do anything I ask. The shelves still are not up in the pantry; the basement window has been broken for months. You're hopeless." Scott shot back, "You never ask. You give orders and more orders, and then you criticize. Why would I do what you want? It's never good enough." One good "blame" deserves another. Patti blames Scott; Scott puts the blame back on Patti. Couple after couple that we counsel make no progress until the partners stop pointing at one another with the message, "We would be fine if you would change." In the 1960s, the psychiatrist Thomas A. Harris set forth his ideas for relationships in his book, *I'm OK—You're OK*. Relationships filled with blame turn his title around. Each partner shouts, "I'm OK, you're not!"

These sad expressions of blame are fueled by feelings ranging from impatience to despair. Bennie Woolley, trainer of the 2009 Kentucky Derby winner Mine That Bird, was incredibly frustrated when his horse lost at Belmont. He blamed the jockey, Calvin Borel. Borel, who had won both the Derby and the Preakness, was crushed with disappointment at not winning all three races of the Triple Crown. He blamed the horse. Others blamed the track for being too sandy and too long. Strong feelings generate blame. Scapegoats are often the consequence of communal guilt or wrath. It seems that many people feel the need to release their feelings by blaming someone.

## Threats and Ultimatums

Our emotions that turn to blame often arise from our needs. We need others, and when our needs are unfulfilled we have emotions and are tempted to blame. The trainer needs the jockey to perform with skill and good judgment; the jockey needs the horse to run at peak level. Patti needs Scott to maintain the house. Scott needs Patti to treat him with respect. We blame if our needs are foiled, but if blame fails to elicit the behavior that would satisfy us, we can be tempted to resort to threats and ultimatums.

A newly engaged couple came to us for counseling. Their problem, claimed Hank, was his fiancée Trish's out-of-control spending: "She doesn't get what a problem this is. Every time we talk about it she says she's sorry, but then she comes home with more stuff." His solution was a threat: "I told her, next time you spend anything we haven't agreed on, I'm taking all your credit cards, and when you need money you have to ask me." Trish fired back, "You're not my father." Hank's exasperation fed his sense of helplessness. Feeling powerless to control his fiancée's spending, he tried to assert power by threatening her. Refusing to submit to his attempt at control, Trish pushed back in anger. Hank's threats failed to produce change in his fiancée's spending or to reduce his frustration. He felt helpless before threatening her and even more helpless afterward.

What Hank didn't do was communicate his feelings. Nor did Trish. He focused on her with threats. She reacted by focusing on him and his assumption of authority over her. The tenor of their interaction changed, however, when Hank shared, "I'm scared. I see you owing more and more money, and I don't know how to stop you." Trish responded, "I'm scared, too. I mean to stop, but then I find myself buying again. I'm afraid you'll get fed up and leave me." They learned with our coaching to listen to what Trish's spending habit was like for each of them. The more Trish listened, the more she was able to trust Hank's commitment and to accept his support. She resolved to explore the feelings that seemed to spur her need to buy. Hank's threats hadn't motivated her. Their honest sharing and mutual understanding did.

> We usually resort to threats out of a sense of weakness and impatience.

We usually resort to threats out of a sense of weakness and impatience. We want to effect change in someone else's behavior, feel helpless to do so, and then decide to use threats. If one threat doesn't work, we often try another and another in a futile escalation. When the Klaffs' teenage son first came home late on a Saturday night, they reminded him of his weekend curfew. When he again arrived late the following Saturday, they threatened him with the loss of his privileges to drive the family car if he came in late again. By the third Saturday, when the teenager tried to sneak in late, his father burst into his room, "You have no respect for this family. You're grounded and if you're ever late again, I'm taking away your cell phone and the keys to the car, and you'll be grounded the entire school year. Otherwise, you'll go to boarding school." Mr. Klaff's threats finally took on a dimension of desperate overkill. When the family turned to us for help, Mr. Klaff had already stepped back from his dire threats. He felt more ineffective than ever with his son, who was on the verge of taunting his father in our presence.

Threats uttered in frustration but not seriously intended or enforced are not taken seriously. The one making them loses respect as he loses control. The father needed to tell his son how sad he felt at the loss of a trusting relationship. The son needed to share his anger with what he considered an unreasonable curfew and the embarrassment he suffered at having to leave friends at such an hour. Dad had to acknowledge his anxieties about his son's safety and his difficulty relaxing until his son was in the house. The son had to respect his father's feelings. Eventually, they made adjustments to the hour of the curfew, and the boy agreed to let his parents know more clearly where he was and with whom. Disputes are not always resolved by honest discussion, but threats, particularly escalating ones, rarely solve anything.

Ultimatums are the last straw of threats. Threats are a warning. We warn, "You do that and there will be consequences." Ultimatums offer a final choice. "Choose drinking or choose the family—one or the other." "Have another affair and it's the end of the marriage." "Attend your classes or you don't live at home." Ultimatums can be effective in calling an individual to serious, responsible behavior. They can motivate a person to look deeply at his behavior by forcing him to choose. Ultimatums need to be made only as a last resort and only if they are meant. Many ultimatums, like many threats, are not intended to be enforced; they are cries of desperation and as such tend only to intensify futility. The words are empty and are easily ignored.

A distraught divorced mother screams at her teenage daughter, "You obey me or you live with your father." She desperately wants her daughter to show respect and to observe her rules, but her ultimatum is not a serious one. It becomes an idle threat since the mother has no intention of enforcing it. As a result, she loses even more respect and control. Threats and ultimatums without follow-through are toothless. They expose the impotence of the one delivering them and actually empower the one receiving them. They contribute to distance between the two parties. Threats and ultimatums uttered without genuine conviction are a waste of words, a waste of energy, and a waste of time. They usually worsen what they attempt to resolve. Meaningful interaction occurs when words mean what they say, when words are truthful expressions of feelings and intentions.

■ F O R   R E F L E C T I O N ■

1. *Blaming is often a knee-jerk defensive reaction. Recall a moment when you blamed someone and why you did so.*

2. *Describe the difference between blaming someone and sharing your feelings about the person's behavior.*

3. *Think of a threat or ultimatum you have expressed toward someone. Now try instead to express the feelings and perceptions that were behind the statement.*

Chapter Thirteen

# *a grab bag of unproductive verbal behaviors*

I like to do all the talking myself. It saves time and prevents arguments.

—Oscar Wilde

Communication that unites individuals in trust and understanding is simple—speak your truth as you know it, and listen to the one speaking. Simple, yes, but difficult. For many reasons you have probably developed verbal habits that hinder you from "saying it like it is," from being simply honest. Some of these ineffective verbal behaviors are the topics of previous chapters: impersonal sharing, withholding silence, lies and exaggerations, questions, judgments, blame, and threats. The list, sadly, could go on and on. Humans have discovered countless ways to speak that are far from simple, direct expressions of their inner thoughts and feelings. We'll conclude this section of the book with a brief discussion of some of the most common forms of unproductive expressions.

## Absolutes and Universals

Truth is said to be the first casualty of war; it is also a casualty of poor communication. Lies, fibs, and exaggerations are not the only behaviors that fail to respect the truth; absolutes and universals show a similar disrespect. A teacher says to a first grader, "You're always jumping up and down." Not true. It might seem to the distracted teacher that the redheaded youngster in the front row is *never* still, but how long, really, could he jump up and down? Jill is not in fact *always* going to the bathroom. Nor is Timmy *always* disrupting the class. A manager of a sales division confronted one of his team: "You are *always* leaving early." A careful review of the employee's time sheets revealed that he was leaving early on average once a week—too often for his manager, but not *always*. A harried mother charged her teenage daughter in our office, "You *never* help around the house." The daughter had no difficulty outlining numerous responsible actions she had performed in the previous two days. The teacher, the manager, and the mother did not intend to distort the truth, but driven by strong feelings they overstated the facts. They might also have been trying to express the great degree to which they were being affected by the others' behaviors and attempting to justify the strength of their feelings. But the recipients will most likely hear an inherently unfair accusation, preventing both understanding and an effective addressing of the problem. Absolutes overstate the facts. They are usually uttered to stress a point but fail to impress precisely because they are inaccurate.

> Truth is said to be the first casualty of war; it is also a casualty of poor communication.

Universals, like absolutes, are statements that allow no exception. Absolutes attempt to make their case by employing "always" and "never." Universals rely on "all" and "every." Like absolutes, universals sacrifice truth for emphasis. "*All* men are afraid of their feelings." "*All* women are too emotional." The "all" can be expressed or implied, "[All] Swedes are unemotional." "[All] Germans are rational." The universal "all" doesn't acknowledge individuality in its sweeping generalization. Bjorn,

Brigitte, and Anika—all the same, no differences. Every Republican is a capitalist. Every Democrat is a tax-spender. Every Southerner is laid back, and every New Yorker is rude. Universals, used casually or dogmatically, ignore evidence of difference, and consequently the speaker sounds ignorant and even prejudiced. Universals do not promote appreciation of the individual or understanding of a group. They also prevent a more personal revelation of the one using such blanket statements.

## Sarcasm

Sarcasm is the intellectual's way of disguising feelings. When you are sarcastic, you channel your irritation, impatience, resentment, jealousy, and anger through your intellect. You don't have to blow up, vent, or scream; you skewer the other with a rapier thrust from a lofty stance. You don't have to stoop to conquer. Churchill was a master of the sarcastic craft. At a dinner, an annoyed Lady Astor snapped at the prime minister, "If you were my husband, I would poison your coffee." Churchill replied, "If I were your husband, I would drink it." No emotional outburst, the insult was delivered by cool and clever sarcasm designed to inflict pain, not to promote a trusting connection.

In one couple's counseling session, a frustrated, lonely woman cried at her partner, "You are so aloof. You think you are so damned smart. I can't stand it when you act like this." Her partner answered icily, "You are so smart you didn't have to go to college." His sarcasm bit into her. He might have thought he had won with his withering retort, but what had he won? Certainly not sympathy or affection. Sarcasm can be an effective defense or attack, but it does real damage to intimacy. Behind the sarcasm are feelings. The quipping partner, in this instance, gradually uncovered long-held distrust, fear of being hurt, and awkwardness in revealing himself. These feelings had hardened into a cynical veneer with sarcasm as part of the defense.

A driven forty-five-year-old executive had a similar cynical style. Her sarcasm kept her colleagues at a distance. While we

> Sarcasm is the intellectual's way of disguising feelings.

were consulting at her company, we watched her clear a group from her office with a sarcastic remark originally attributed to Jane Austen: "You have delighted us long enough." This executive is feared in the company and has few friends. Sarcasm doesn't win hearts or even minds.

## Teasing

Teasing is sarcasm's genial twin. Sarcasm thrusts with hurtful wit; teasing pokes fun. It can demonstrate playful affection. It can make someone laugh. Teasing that enhances intimacy is sparked by and imbued with affection. Ronny, a jovial woman in her fifties, told us about her husband's teasing. "Chris makes me laugh out loud. He knows me so well. At a charity auction last week he caught my eye from across the room and did a quick imitation of the way I was talking to one of the hosts. I had to keep myself from bursting out laughing." We learned from Ronny that Chris is frequently the target of his own humor. Maybe being able to laugh at oneself is the mark of a genuinely inoffensive teaser.

> Teasing is sarcasm's genial twin.

Teasing can be unproductive, however, and hurtful when it goes "too far," when it starts to prick instead of please. Laura, an accountant at a large firm, described teasing that is devoid of humor. One colleague seems to have radar for her vulnerabilities. "I hate it. She teases me about my accent, my weight, and my clothes. If I react, I look like I'm too sensitive. But if I go along I'm afraid of encouraging her." Sometimes teasing is a coward's way of criticizing. Possibly the colleague hurting Laura teases when in fact she wants to disparage Laura. Yet if she were questioned, she could defend by exclaiming, "No! I love your accent. I was only joking." Humor can lighten the tone and provide comic relief, but it can disguise a superior or critical attitude as well. Make sure you are not finding fault when you are tempted to tease.

## Talking without Feelings

Some people don't refer to feelings at all. They have opinions on any topic, thoughts on any issue, and a willingness to proffer them. But their feelings are as remote as their fluency in Swahili. They are ignorant of their own feelings and uncomfortable with anyone else's. Two sisters in our office attempted to talk about their brother's recent announcement that he was gay. Alma looked impatient when her sister Margot began to cry. Alma looked actually panicked when, through her tears, Margot asked Alma how she felt. Alma snapped, "It is what it is." Margot persisted, "But I need to talk about it. We need to know what we feel before we can talk to him." Alma started to leave and said, "This is futile. For heaven's sakes, get a grip." Sadly, Alma was right: the conversation was futile. They couldn't talk because Alma was completely unwilling or unable to cope with her sister's feelings or to admit her own.

Personal meeting is rendered impossible when the feelings underlying questions, opinions, and thoughts are ignored or denied. A cousin in a rather skeptical tone asked us at a family gathering, "Do you think therapy really accomplishes anything?" When we explored what she meant by the question, she shifted her approach. "It's just that I think a lot of people are too needy." We tried to focus on her meaning, but she began to discuss an article that she had read. "Its point is that not all kinds of therapy are effective." Trying to connect with this cousin was both frustrating and unpleasant. She either had no idea what she was feeling about psychotherapy (or us practicing it) or she had no intention of admitting her feelings.

People who won't acknowledge feelings tend to talk *at* others. They talk from their heads without revealing any emotions that might be behind their thoughts. At best, they engage in an exchange of ideas and information; at worst they indulge in monologues or provoke pointless arguments. Intimate verbal encounter relies on individuals delving beneath the surface of their thoughts.

> People who won't acknowledge feelings tend to talk at others.

It requires the speaker to willingly own his feelings and to express them. Conversation that is restricted to thoughts might only achieve some limited goals—intimacy is not one of them.

## Verbal Tics

Most of us develop verbal mannerisms. These don't serve any productive purpose and often foster unproductive communication. Verbal tics don't make our oral expression more understandable, and they grate on our listeners' ears. Unfortunately, we are seldom aware of these verbal mannerisms. Others suffer them silently or try to ignore them.

Some tics deflect the listeners' attention and may even harm their opinion of the speaker. Caroline Kennedy probably had said, "you know," unthinkingly until she ran for Hillary Clinton's vacated senate seat. Her candidacy and her image were dealt a blow when she uttered her habitual "you know" 144 times in an 8,500-word interview. Punctuating their narratives with the word "like," many teenagers strain adults' patience and hinder their ability to take seriously what the teenagers are saying. "So, like he came into the cafeteria and I was like, who is this dude? Like I had never seen him before. And he was like just standing there. Latisha and I were just like amazed." The ABC golf commentator Ken Venturi distracts some of his audience with the habit of introducing his remarks with "I'll tell you what . . ." "I'll tell you what, golfers are in better shape than they used to be." "I'll tell you what, these greens are fast." "I'll tell you what, Tiger's short game is amazing." A fan would be justified in saying, "Spare us the 'I'll tell you what' and just tell me." Television political pundits have begun to preface their observations with "Look." "Look, if the president wants to succeed on this issue . . ." "Look, the election results are definitely suspicious." The word "look" is meant to direct our attention to what is going to be said, but it only distracts us with the unnecessary word itself.

Some verbal tics jar the listener by seemingly calling for a response. A loquacious gardener we know interrupts his narratives frequently with, "Am I right, Doc?" We've toyed with the thought of startling him by actually answering the apparently rhetorical question. Some people can't seem to express themselves without asking, "You know what I mean?" or "Does that make sense?" Most of the French do the same with "n'est-ce pas?" These remarks might be invitations to the listener to comment, but more often they degenerate into thoughtless tics that do little or nothing to promote positive interaction.

"To be honest" is another disconcerting verbal habit. Was the speaker being dishonest prior to announcing, "To be honest, I've never liked mushrooms," "To be honest, I hate reality shows"? Some individuals need to stress their veracity: "To be *perfectly* honest, I think bottled water is a waste of money." The verbal tic "I'm sorry, but . . ." seems actually to *be* dishonest. Is the speaker really sorry when she states, "I'm sorry, but I think the way the president is handling the economy is outrageous"? She sounds angry, not apologetic. "I'm sorry, but I don't think teenagers should be allowed to drive." Adamant or convinced, perhaps, but not sorry. Some verbal mannerisms seem less about being honest than about being self-protective. The preface, "If you don't mind my saying so . . ." tacitly tells the listener, "You surely can't object to my remark or react against me." "If you don't mind my saying, you tended to dominate the meeting."

"I'm only telling you this for your own good" and "with all due respect" serve a similar goal of preempting an adverse reaction. "I'm not the only one who thinks so," added onto a critical comment, attempts to remove the focus of responsibility from the speaker, but also tosses in some added emphasis. "You have been very opinionated at the book club. I'm not the only one who thinks so." In essence, "There! I don't stand alone. I have unnamed troops to back me up." Such phrases do not foster constructive conversations in any relationship.

We become so deaf to our own verbal tics that we can forget that words matter. But our words do matter. They impart meaning. They convey our thoughts and our innermost sentiments. Mindless and even irresponsible verbal mannerisms offend by making words meaningless.

## Giving Advice

Sarcasm puts people down by attempting to hurt; giving advice drives people away by trying to help. When you advise someone, you don't offer yourself, you provide answers. You stand outside and, wittingly or unwittingly, above others and tell them what they should or should not do. A friend tells you that she is having trouble with her three-year-old. You tell her, "You have to be more (or less) strict," "You have to take her to this child psychologist I know," or "You have to give her more attention." There! You've been a good friend. Next? Your sister informs you that Mother is driving her crazy. You are quick to advise, "Just ignore her," "Call her more often," "You should be more patient with her," or "You have to stick up for yourself." The message is that you know how to handle your mother and your sister doesn't. Why doesn't she just act like you?

> Sarcasm puts people down by attempting to hurt; giving advice drives people away by trying to help.

People have problems; you have solutions. If only they would listen, you could help. But most people want to be heard. They want the opportunity to vent or to sort out their feelings or options. They need space to voice their turmoil—space that a good listener can provide. As a brilliant, successful executive going through difficulties in his marriage told us, "I can't talk to anyone about this, especially my family. They all have advice. They love me. They want what's best for me. But they can't stop themselves from giving their opinion of what I should do." People who give advice block deeper communication between themselves and others by making people feel as though only their problems have been heard, not their feelings. Advice givers share their problem-solving skills or knowledge but they disguise their concern and care.

The goals of interpersonal interaction are intimacy, understanding, and authentic connection. These aims are not easily realized. They require a commitment to honest and responsible sharing. The unproductive behaviors that we have discussed are hurdles impeding the way to accomplishing these goals.

■ F O R   R E F L E C T I O N ■

1. *How often in a day do you think you use absolutes and universals? Jot down a few you have made recently. What were you feeling when you said them?*

2. *When are you sarcastic? Are you feeling defensive? Are you frustrated but reluctant to state your feelings of anger or frustration directly?*

3. *Heighten your awareness of verbal tics. Do you hear them in others? Do you think you can recognize your own?*

4. *Do you know what you are feeling when you give advice? Are you comfortable hearing someone else's plight without having to provide a solution?*

Part Three

Chapter Fourteen

# *communicating*
# *effectively*

Love takes off the masks that we fear we cannot live without and know we cannot live within.

—James Baldwin, *The Fire Next Time*

By this point, you may be disheartened. If asked to admit which of the previously outlined poor communication patterns you have employed, you might proclaim, "All of them." Possibly you can identify your proclivity to speak impersonally, judge others, withhold by silence, or attack with blame. You might be able to confess to fibs and exaggerations while acknowledging any number of annoying verbal tics. But awareness of your offenses is an essential step to correcting them. So, with heightened awareness of your communication misdeeds, you are ready to learn new ways of expressing yourself, ways more promising for achieving satisfying connection with others. Take heart by taking aim at ineffective verbal patterns and by acquiring new, more positive skills.

## Step One: Stop to Reflect

You can't give what you haven't got. Unless you are aware of your feelings and perceptions, you can't share them. Likewise, if you don't know what your needs are, you won't be able to state them. Without being mindful of your intentions in speaking, you are like a loose cannon firing without clear direction as you speak without conscious reason. You must be clear within yourself first if you want to have a chance of being transparent to others. Effective communication with others relies on successful communication with yourself.

Unless you are aware of your feelings and perceptions, you can't share them.

So, for example, before you speak to your partner about his behavior, you must stop to reflect. Listen to yourself to identify the way that the behavior is affecting you. Let's say you are responding to his failure to exercise:

What are you feeling?
    Are you impatient? anxious? fearful? resentful?

What do you need?
    To be free from fear regarding his health? to feel
        more physically attracted to him? to have him
        as an active biking or hiking partner?

How do you perceive his lack of exercise?
    Does it seem due to laziness? busyness? fear of fail-
        ure? lack of confidence or discipline?

What are you intending by speaking?
    Are you genuinely concerned for his health and
        want to prevent illness or a heart attack? Do
        you subtly intend to appear superior?
    Are you attempting to get back at him for critical
        remarks that he has directed at you?
    Do you want him to understand you, or are you
        trying to change him?

Only when you are alert to what is happening within you can you offer yourself to your partner. Without this awareness you might easily "act out" by suggesting, nagging, or even screaming. Sharing yourself openly and responsibly in a way that your partner can hear requires effort. You don't have to be so self-aware just to talk. If you want to make yourself genuinely visible, however, you will have to reflect on your feelings, needs, perceptions, and intentions before you share.

Step one in good communication is stepping back, to become aware of yourself, to give yourself a moment to realize what you want to say and why. Shooting from the hip is quick and easy—it can inaccurately even be called spontaneous. It isn't. Spontaneity involves freedom. Speaking without reflection is often a reaction triggered by unacknowledged feelings. Our feelings in such reactions control us and our remarks. We are not free when our feelings rule us.

## Step Two: Know Your Intentions

In the preceding example of speaking to your partner regarding his lack of exercise, let's say that you have taken the time to ponder why you wish to talk to him and what you want to say. The "why" is your intention; the "what" is your feelings, needs, and perceptions. On reflection, suppose you realize that your intention is to motivate him to join a gym and to begin regular workouts. You become aware that to accomplish your goal you are inclined to be indirect by remarking, "You're looking heavy," or, even less directly, "I read an article that said that men over forty who don't exercise at least three times a week are 50 percent more susceptible to heart attacks than men who do." But you catch yourself and realize that, even though you want him to exercise, the best communication is the most direct and personal. Instead of trying to motivate indirectly, you decide to be honest. You tell him, "I want you to exercise regularly." You've been direct. You've owned up to your desire for him to act.

Then you realize that telling him what you want from him and for him is only part of what is happening within you. Though you don't deny at all your desire for him to exercise, you have to step back again to reflect on the feelings and needs that are prompting you to focus on this issue. You recalibrate your intentions. Now you want to share yourself more completely with your partner. Your intention is to open up to him, to make yourself known to him by sharing what is happening within you regarding his lack of exercise:

■ I feel anxious when I see you putting on weight and not exercising.

■ I worry that you could have a heart attack.

■ I feel disappointed when I see you gaining weight and sitting around on weekends.

■ I loved your look when you were muscle-toned.

■ I need to see you looking healthy.

■ I need us to be active partners.

In this way you have made *yourself* visible to him and offered yourself, your feelings, and needs. Transparency, revealing to him the truth within you, is now your chief intention. You hope that he loves you enough to listen, to empathize with what it is like for you to see him heavier and sedentary. For his sake you hope he would be motivated to take better care of himself. You want him to look good, to be healthy, to exercise, but most of all you want to be honest with him and be known by him. More than to get him to exercise or to do or be anything, your prime intention in sharing is to reveal yourself to him.

In other circumstances, your intention in speaking will not always be to make yourself transparent. But when you realize that you want to be open and honest with your employee, friend, relative, or child, it is imperative that you keep your intentions in focus and not drift off to less productive behaviors. Make sure that your words are true to your intention.

## Step Three: Start by Saying "I"

In order to share yourself, your focus has to be on you. You use the personal pronoun "I." "I feel irritated." "I need more downtime." "I realize that you are tapping your foot." Using the pronoun "I" isn't egotistical; it is appropriate to direct your focus to what *you* are saying. You can't say what you are feeling by avoiding "I" and using the pronouns "we," "one," "you," or "it."

Sharing yourself is not the same as talking *about* yourself.

Harry wants to share himself with Josh. "Your problem, Josh, is you work too hard." What happened to Harry? He didn't share himself. He focused on Josh: "Your problem, Josh . . ." To share himself, Harry would have to put his attention on himself by saying "I." "I feel frustrated when you say you can't take the boat out because you have to work." The pronoun "I" enables personal sharing. *I* am going to share what *I* am feeling, needing, observing. I say "I" because it's the proper pronoun to designate that *I* am speaking and focusing on sharing myself.

It is important to keep in mind here that sharing yourself is not the same as talking *about* yourself. Sharing yourself means that you offer what is happening within you—your feelings primarily, but also your needs, perceptions, and intentions as well as your hopes, beliefs, and thoughts. In order to share yourself, you have to center your attention on your inner world and then make yourself as transparent, as visible, to another as you are able. Merely talking *about* yourself requires less awareness and risks less, even though you still use the pronoun "I." When you talk about yourself, you can pick and choose what you tell about yourself. You can relate an incident that reflects favorably on you, "I was happy to give a hundred dollars to charity," and omit the time when you screamed at the driver whose car braked abruptly in front of yours. You can tell the story about your childhood, the one that elicits admiration, and skip any mention of your failures and *faux pas*. Talking about yourself can be a sincere revelation that allows you to be known, but it can also be manipulative, designed for effect. It can be boastful or self-deprecating, tiresome or self-absorbed. Whether you are enhancing a story or indulging in a monologue, talking about yourself is different from sharing your feelings. So, in order to make yourself immediately present to another person, start by saying "I" and keep your focus on what is happening *within* you.

## Step Four: Say What You Are Feeling

In order to share your feelings, after you start with the word
"I," follow it with the word "feel" to direct your attention to the
emotions that you intend to express. Harry says to Josh, "I feel."
The word "feel" is followed by the emotion that Harry is communicating: "I feel frustrated." Sounds logical. Harry feels the
emotion of frustration. But to be able to share this emotion,
Harry has to know it. Many people are unaware of their feelings, and even if they have some sense of what is happening
inside them emotionally, they can't put that vague sense into
words. Often in counseling or consulting we ask an individual,
"What are you feeling?" only to hear back, "Nothing. I'm not
feeling anything." *That's not possible.* We can't *not* feel any more
than we can't *not* think. We feel; we think. Most of us can readily identify our thoughts but not so easily our feelings. In order
to be able to relate your feelings, you have to tune into them.
This will require listening more closely to your emotions and
learning to articulate them. You might make it a practice to stop
three times a day—in the morning, afternoon, and evening—
and register the feelings you have had to that point in the day.
You jot down how you felt first thing in the morning: eager or
anxious about the day's projects, grateful for the weather, peaceful waiting for a bus, or frustrated with the subway. At midday
you identify feelings you have experienced throughout the
morning but possibly have not registered. You do the same in
the evening, looking back over the afternoon. Focusing on your
feelings and identifying them with words will heighten your
awareness. Remember, you can't share your inner emotional
world unless you know it.

Beware of the sloppy habit of saying, "I feel," followed by
the word "that"—"I feel that . . ." The insertion of "that" shifts
your focus away from self-revelation. When you say, "I feel frustrated," or, "I feel excited," your words reveal you. When you
say the words "I feel that," you tell your listener about him or
her or about others. "I feel that you are misguided." "I feel that
you are selfish." "I feel that they never give me a chance." "I feel
that children should be seen and not heard." The word "like"
after "I feel" similarly directs your focus away from your

feelings. "I feel like you never say what you mean." "I feel like this country is going in the wrong direction." It is not difficult to say, "I feel." It is exacting, though, to identify and articulate feelings. Some people are so unaccustomed to voicing their feelings that they will need to learn a vocabulary of emotions. (See the list of feelings in the Appendix.) If you have difficulty finding language to express your feelings, start with general words like "good" and "bad"—"I feel good" or "I feel bad." Or try spatial terms: "I feel close" or "I feel distant." With some concentration and effort, you can learn the language that describes your inner world of feelings. Just as with any foreign language, if you didn't grow up speaking it, you can still master it with practice.

## Step Five: Identify Your Perceptions

You have begun your personal sharing with "I" then the word "feel" followed by an emotion, such as "hurt," "sad," "delighted," "fearful." In the next step you provide the reason for your feeling. Simply stating your emotions doesn't make you fully visible or transparent. "I feel anxious" reveals your emotional state, but you could be anxious for many reasons: your financial situation, a report you have to give, a doctor's appointment, or a court summons you have received. To reveal yourself fully, connect the expression of your feelings with the reason for them. "I feel anxious because I felt a lump in my breast." "I feel excited because my best friend is coming to visit." "I feel discouraged because I can't lose weight." You make yourself visible to another by starting with the pronoun "I," adding a feeling, and concluding with the reason for the feeling:

I feel _____(*emotion*) because _____(*reason for your feeling*).

Frequently, the reason for your feeling will be your perception of an individual, an object, or an event.

So what is a perception? First we define it, then provide some examples. A perception is a sense experience that gains meaning when you interpret it. It is something you see or hear or touch to which you attribute meaning. For instance, you see your son playing a video game at 8:00 p.m., a time designated

A perception is a sense experience that gains meaning when you interpret it.

for his homework. You could perceive that behavior as defiance of your rules or even your authority. Your feeling then might be irritation or anger. On the other hand, you could perceive that he has gotten so absorbed that he has forgotten the time. You could feel impatient if you perceive that this forgetful behavior is happening frequently. If you see his behavior as a sign of unhappiness, however, you then might feel concerned. Your feeling, you see, depends on your perception—the way that you *perceive* his behavior.

A friend fails to respond to an invitation to a party. If you perceive his non-response as lack of respect for you, you would probably feel hurt or resentment. If you perceive his lack of response as shyness, you could feel sympathetic. Your feelings are not governed by another's behavior but by the way that you interpret that behavior. You have every right to your emotions and to your perceptions. But good communication requires that you accept that *your* feelings are based on *your* perceptions. You don't have a certainty of what is the fact, what is true, even what is real. You have *your* perception and that perception is *your* interpretation. Share your feelings and express the reason for them honestly, even forcefully, but as a statement of what is happening within you, not as a judgment of what you declare to be objectively true.

## Step Six: Express Your Perceptions

Compare these statements:

- I felt bewildered when I heard you tell Tara that she is too talkative. That seemed cruel.

- I felt bewildered at your cruelty to Tara.

The first statement expresses your feelings and perceptions. You were bewildered at a behavior that you perceived as cruel. By contrast, in the second statement you are being judgmental by labeling your friend's behavior as "cruel."

In the first statement your use of the word "seemed" indicates that you are sharing *your perception* of his remark. You are disclosing yourself, not defining your friend. When you use the word "seem" you point to your observation as you have interpreted it. "It seems to me that your remark was cruel." Your friend might have a different perception. He might say, "It seemed to me the comment was playful," or, "It seemed to me I was letting her know as a friend that she was talking a lot." The issue here is not semantics, merely to do with choice of words; the issue is intention. Are you trying to share yourself, admitting to your emotion and your perception? If so, the word "seems" helps you to do that. Or are you attempting to define another's reality? Many arguments are fueled by the participants' determination to define the other and to be "right" themselves.

Imagine two roommates trying to understand each other talking this way: The first one says, "I'm angry because you're so obsessed with neatness." (Fact!) "I'm fed up with your being such a slob." (Fact!) A productive conversation might ensue if each of the combatants stopped labeling and instead shared themselves: "I felt angry when you started straightening up my desk. It seemed picky." "I felt frustrated when you left the mail in a pile on the desk. I couldn't find my bank statement." Maybe the accuser is sensitive because she fears being controlled by her roommate. Maybe the accused is easily distracted by disorder. Each might profit from listening to herself more responsibly and to the other less defensively. Satisfactory interaction is far more likely when the individuals stop judging and humbly start sharing.

"When" is another word that you can use to direct your feelings and perceptions to a specific moment when they occurred within you. "*When* I saw the pile of mail on the desk, I felt angry." "*When* I heard you call her talkative, I felt angry." The word "when" can help you to concentrate, to locate the exact incident that triggered your feeling. It can facilitate your sharing, making it precise and, therefore, not only more accurate but also more likely to be accepted. If you said, "I felt hurt when you didn't write a card for our anniversary," you would have a better chance of being heard accurately than if you said, "I felt hurt that our anniversary doesn't mean much to you." The word "when" identifies the moment a feeling occurred: "When you told that ethnic joke, I felt mortified." By saying "when" you avoid grand general statements such as, "I hate the way you act at parties." The word "seems" reminds you, the speaker, that you have perceptions, not objective facts. The word "when" limits your feelings to the instant that they happened.

The words you choose matter. They enable you to convey the inner mystery of yourself, first of all to yourself and then to those to whom you choose to be transparent. Saying "I," finding the right words that capture your emotions, admitting your perceptions with "seem" and "when," all serve you in your efforts to communicate effectively.

## ■  FOR  REFLECTION  ■

1.  We believe that the steps to communicating effectively are:

    Step one—Stop to reflect.

    Step two—Know your intentions.

    Step three—Start by saying "I."

    Step four—Say what you are feeling.

    Step five—Identify your perceptions.

    Step six—Express your perceptions.

    On which of these steps are you most likely to stumble?

2.  With whom would you most like to communicate more effectively?

3.  In what settings will you have to work the hardest to communicate more effectively?

# Chapter Fifteen

# *examples of effective communication*

To this day, I find it hard to gaze directly at people like Hassan, people who mean every word they say. . . . And that's the thing about people who mean every thing they say. They think everyone else does too.

—Khaled Hosseini, *The Kite Runner*

We learn best by example. So this chapter presents examples of individuals trying to communicate in a variety of situations. First, we show them coping ineffectively and communicating unproductively with themselves and with others. These people are burdened with misguided intentions and unexpressed emotions. Then we suggest the steps they need to take in order to communicate in a constructive manner. Finally, we depict simple examples of individuals who impressed us with spontaneous, authentic communication skills.

## Examples of Unproductive Talking

### *Lucas and Self-Talk*

Lucas, who six months previously had graduated from college, tried to describe his emotions. "I am such a loser. I'm going nowhere. All of my friends have gotten jobs and their own apartments. Their parents have supported them. Mine don't get how hard it is." Lucas is overwhelmed by feelings of discouragement and fear, but his self-critical talk is further deepening his confusion. He had taken out massive loans to complete his last two years of college. Two months before completing his senior year, he had applied for jobs but had found nothing. He had no prospects, no money, and huge loans to pay off. His parents were pressuring him to pick a date when he would move out of their house, start an internship, or volunteer—anything other than be immobile and isolated. He didn't understand himself, and he didn't know what to say to his parents.

Lucas needed to talk primarily to sort himself out. He said he felt "lost." As he talked, he identified other feelings: feeling overwhelmed, baffled at what steps to take, and even helpless. He recognized that, though he was resentful of his parents' pressure to set deadlines, he was more sad that he was disappointing them. He admitted that he felt depressed and was able to connect his depression with his isolating behavior.

By admitting his feelings, Lucas's mood lifted slightly. He realized that conceding to his desire to withdraw not only intensified his parents' demands but also exacerbated his feelings of hopelessness. Gradually, Lucas forced himself out of immobility and isolation. He initiated daily workouts at the gym. He began to socialize with the friends whom he had been avoiding. He talked with his parents, who had become less critical as they saw him taking action, and he renewed his efforts to get a job. Lucas had been dominated by moods that stemmed from unemployment and unexpressed feelings. Opening up to himself was the first step toward hope and toward interacting with others.

## Reflective Process

Before clarifying his feelings, Lucas had been saying to himself:
> I'm a loser.
> I'm going nowhere.
> My parents don't get how hard this is.

He reflects and identifies his feelings:
> I feel overwhelmed.
> I feel baffled.
> I feel depressed.

He admits his feelings while refusing to allow them to produce self-defeating accusations and comparisons that result in hopelessness:
> I feel sad and afraid that I won't be able to find a job.
> I feel depressed and I want to withdraw.
> I feel sluggish so it's hard to get out and exercise.
> I feel confused that the job search is so difficult.

## Productive Expression

With knowledge of his own feelings Lucas can express them directly to his parents:
> I regret that you have been worried. I've been totally stuck, but I'm clarifying what I have to do.
> I felt so down that I felt paralyzed. I know I've strained your patience, but I hope you'll keep being patient while I figure this out.

### Mr. Dennison, Grant, and Criticism

The Dennisons' oldest child, Grant, is, his father says, "just plain stubborn." Mr. Dennison catalogued his criticisms of Grant: "When the family goes on a car trip, before we are even in the car, Grant starts an argument about who gets to sit in the front seat. He makes school mornings a nightmare. If we toast

bagels for breakfast, Grant decides he wants cereal. He'll pour a
bowl of cereal, and then ask his brother for half of his bagel."
When they pick a movie, a computer game, or sport, "it always
has to be Grant's way or no way. He has no consideration for his
brothers. It's all about him." Grant's father doesn't know where
or how to begin talking to Grant.

Yet his son desperately needs his father's guidance. What
Grant does not need to hear are the judgments his father has
formed. Grant probably, deep down, feels that he is bad or infe-
rior. Most likely he's unhappy and acts in a way that draws negative attention from everyone at home. Judgments of Grant
from his dad as "obstinate" or "selfish" would serve only to
cement Grant's poor self-image. To talk in an effective way with
Grant, Mr. Dennison has some work to do first.

### Reflective Process

Mr. Dennison needs first to recognize how critical he is
being of Grant:
   Grant makes school mornings a nightmare.
   Grant has to have his own way.
   Grant has no consideration for his brothers.
   It's all about him.

He has to identify his own feelings and to recognize that he
has been acting out of these feelings by being excessively
critical:
   I feel angry.
   I feel impatient.
   I feel resentful.

But he also feels:
   Love for Grant.
   Sympathy for Grant.
   Fear that Grant will always be unhappy.

### Productive Expression

Recognizing that he has to control his feelings and not act
out of them by criticizing Grant, Mr. Dennison can now talk
more responsibly to his son:

> I need it quiet in the morning, so I appreciate how
> quickly you responded when Mom asked you
> to keep it down.
> I feel impatient when I have to tell you more than
> once to get dressed for school.
> I trust you, Grant. I can see that you're trying not
> to get into an argument.
> I feel sad when I see you angry again.

By sharing his feelings with Grant, Mr. Dennison is able to reveal himself to his son. He allows his son to get to know him, to experience his frustration but also his tenderness. He relates to his son his own needs while communicating his need for Grant to act more responsibly. His words demonstrate reasonable expectations and genuine care rather than further disapproval.

### Brian, Arthur, and Judgments

Brian, a mid-level manager who leads a team of five people in a small company, grumbles about a new employee, Arthur. Arthur had been hired to fill a particular business need, but socially he wasn't working well with the team that Brian had formed. "I thought when we hired him that he was just a quiet guy, but now I think we picked the wrong person." Brian began to analyze Arthur: "I think he actually doesn't know how to behave in a work environment. If I ask him a question about a report, he keeps staring at his computer. He never makes eye contact. He won't acknowledge e-mails." Over time, Brian's perceptions of Arthur hardened into judgments. "He's a nut case. He's not just immature; he's weird."

Brian's judgments of Arthur negated any chance that he could manage him in a way that benefited Arthur or the team. Beneath Brian's judgments were feelings and needs that he had to recognize before he could confront Arthur directly. Ironically, Brian's judgments were causing him to withdraw from Arthur. The less he talked to Arthur the more his conviction grew that Arthur was weird. Judgments have a way of reinforcing themselves and proving to the judge that they are true.

### Reflective Process

Brian needs to recognize his judgments of Arthur:
He's a nut case.
He's not just immature; he's weird.

He has to acknowledge that he's feeling:
Frustrated with himself for hiring Arthur.
Irritated that he has to confront an adult about fundamental social skills.
Hopeful that Arthur can learn.
Encouraged that things can change.

He has to recognize his needs:
For his team to function smoothly.
For Arthur to interact more with his peers.
For Arthur to answer e-mails in a timely manner.

### Productive Expression

After identifying the feelings and needs he has regarding Arthur, Brian can speak directly to him:
When I asked you for that report yesterday, I felt aggravated that you didn't even look at me.
I need you to check your e-mails regularly and to return them promptly. I want clients to know that they have access to us and that we'll respond to them right away.
You seem withdrawn from the guys in the office. I'm concerned about how you are feeling here.
You seem withdrawn from the guys in the office. I'd like to see you out of your cubicle and interacting more. Everybody needs to know what part of the program you're working on.

Brian might eventually decide that Arthur is not suited to the job or to the team. But as manager, Brian's responsibility is to express his feelings, needs, and expectations clearly. If Arthur cannot or will not respond effectively, then Brian can communicate to him his decision to let him go. If, on the other hand,

Arthur becomes a productive team player, Brian can be gratified that his bracing confrontation has proved effective.

## Sue, Leah, and Giving Advice

Sue is on her way into New York City to "have a talk" with her younger sister, Leah. She has their conversation planned out in detail. After four years of watching her sister flounder as an actress/model/waitress/bartender, she plans to address her sister's income, health insurance, apartment, and her parents' financial support. "I think she needs to know that we are all worried about her and that she's not making it as an actress and has to get serious about work." Sue is not really going to "have a talk"; she is going to lecture her sister. She is not going to share herself. She is going to speak for a group, presumably of family members: "We are all worried about her." Her intended words provide little assurance that her trip will be successful. Leah is about to be confronted with a stern sermon, one that supposedly represents the concerns of the entire family.

### Reflective Process

For the visit to have any chance of being a satisfying meeting, Sue will have to consider her intentions:
Get her sister to change.
Have her sister agree that it would be best to
change and get a "real" job.
Tell her sister to give up her dream of being an
actress or model.

She has to contemplate why she needs her sister to take such a course of action:
She needs her parents to not be burdened with
Leah's finances.
She needs to be relieved of the anxiety she feels
about Leah.
She needs Leah to be safe.

She has to reflect on her feelings regarding her sister's situation:
She's scared that Leah will always be dependent.

She feels exasperated with Leah's seeming ignorance of Sue's fears.

She feels resentful that Leah is taking money that
would eventually be willed to Sue's children.

### Productive Expression

When she does intend to share herself, Sue might offer:
I feel concerned for you. I don't know if you are
eating properly since you have no income.

I'm worried that you could get depressed if you
don't get a part soon.

I resent that our parents are supporting you.

After considering her feelings, needs, and intentions, Sue
might resolve to modify her plan. She would probably not
appreciate her sister telling *her* what to do—why would Leah
respond differently? Sue might have to admit that her need is to
lessen her own anxiety about her sister's welfare. Perhaps she'll
become aware that she needs to talk to her parents more than
she needs to talk to Leah. If she does talk to Leah, she has to talk
for herself. Speaking for "all of us" loads the deck against her
sister and gives Leah no opportunity to respond to the family
members not present.

Leah might not have empathy for Sue's feelings, but that's not
in Sue's control. What she has in her control is recognition of her
motives in talking to her sister, acceptance of her needs, and honest expression of her feelings towards Leah. Maybe Leah can then
respond honestly and the two could meet as equals—a meeting
not likely to occur under Sue's original plan.

### Murphy and Sarcasm

"I'm a cynic," Murphy proclaims. He claims this label,
apparently, with pride. His wife, Marissa, snarls at the boast.
"He's got a sarcastic remark for everything and everybody."
When his brother made a good deal selling a piece of real estate,
Murphy observed, "He thinks he's Donald Trump." When
Marissa posed in her new outfit for a Super Bowl party, Murphy
acidly remarked, "You know you're not going to be *performing*

during halftime." He dismissed a colleague with the comment, "He's not the sharpest tool in the box."

Murphy defends his sarcasm, maintaining that people just don't get his "sense of humor." But his cynical view of the people who surround him leaves him lonely. In order for Murphy to be less lonely, he will have to be more honest and more vulnerable. He will have to admit to feelings—not an easy task for someone who has buried them since childhood to avoid feeling hurt. No man can be happy as an island. Murphy sits alone looking forlornly at the world or stepping into it armed with cynicism. His misery is self-inflicted. Murphy has to open up and open out.

It is not easy to discard a habitual way of acting, especially if the behavior has become a defining characteristic. But Murphy's actions are self-destructive. Breaking these cynical habits will be difficult but can prove to be life-changing.

For Murphy to make a connection with the people he cares for, he will have to be honest with himself.

### Reflective Process

Murphy has to recognize his sarcastic comments:
"He thinks he's Donald Trump."
"You're not going to be *performing* at halftime."
"He's not the sharpest tool in the box."

He needs to identify his feelings related to his brother:
Envy at his success.
Admiration of his success.
Hurt dating from childhood.
Insecurity about his own success.

He needs to own his feelings toward his wife:
Jealousy of her freedom.
Fear of her criticism.
Embarrassment with her style of dress.
Pride in her looks.

## Productive Expression

When Murphy is able to honestly identify feelings rather than automatically resort to sarcasm, he can share with his brother and wife in a way that makes him more visible and less hurtful. He can say:

I envy your success.
Maybe I've always envied you, but I feel hurt that
      you don't respect me.
I feel inadequate at parties especially if I have to
      resist being sarcastic.
I admire your ease with people.
I love the way you look.

Sarcasm and cynicism have left Murphy isolated. By honest self-revelation, he can stop driving away people whom he loves and needs. Instead he can discover the joy of forming trusting and satisfying relationships.

### Jan, Her Lawyer, and Questions

Jan peppers her lawyer with questions: "When do the documents have to be ready? If we get them in today, will the court process them right away? What rights do I have in the meantime? Why didn't you file the other ones last week?" Obviously, when Jan meets with her lawyer, she is seeking information and guidance, but Jan's stream of questions bombards the lawyer into silence and probably into his own feelings of irritation.

Jan has intense feelings of anxiety and needs information, reassurance, and action from her attorney. Allowing these feelings to get the best of her, she asks a flurry of questions that could provoke the lawyer into a defensive reaction. Her feelings would then be exacerbated and her needs left unmet. Effective meetings with her lawyer require that she channel her emotions into clear, direct statements of her feelings and her needs. Jan's lawyer might not change simply because Jan does. He might have been taciturn and defensive long before he met Jan. But slowing down to express herself more deliberately will provide Jan a better chance of being respected and being heard.

## Reflective Process

In order to have a more satisfying session with her attorney, Jan needs to "hold it" and identify her feelings to herself:
I feel anxious that I could lose my house.
I feel concerned that the lawyer is not aware of the
    urgency of the situation.
I feel confused as to my legal rights.

Jan also has to reflect on her needs:
I need this work done effectively.
I need these documents completed right away.
I need clarification.

## Productive Expression

Once she has identified what she needs and what she is feeling, Jan can share with the lawyer:
I feel concerned that you might not be aware of the
    urgency of my case. I felt this concern when
    you didn't file the papers last week.
I need to know how the court proceeds and what
    timeline I can expect.
I am very anxious that I might lose my house.

### Claire, Victor, and Blaming

"You promised me that if ever there was friction between us and your parents, you would always stand by me. So when your father said our house was overpriced and I disagreed, why did you tell me to drop it? If you had taken my side we wouldn't have a problem. You make me feel like a witch." Claire blames Victor for the way that she feels. You can imagine Victor excusing himself by accusing her, "You were going on and on." Their argument, in turn, could go on and on. To have a more productive impact on Victor, Claire has to resist using language to blame. To do so, she has to take some time for reflection, and then share her thoughts with Victor. Claire's honest sharing does not guarantee that Victor will listen or that he will reflect on his behavior, at least not immediately. But speaking the truth as responsibly as possible can strengthen her self-respect and invite Victor's understanding. It might also invite him to look at his own feelings that lie beneath his dismissive remark to Claire.

### Reflective Process

Claire has to reflect on her feelings:
> Hurt that Victor did not stand up for her.
> Embarrassment at being told to "drop it."
> Fear of not being accepted by Victor's family.
> Resentment of her father-in-law for his remarks about the house's value.

She has to identify her needs:
> For Victor's support.
> For Victor's parents to see their son respect his wife's opinions.
> For Victor to be assertive with his father.

### Productive Expression

After reflection on all that is happening within her, Claire is ready to share rather than blame:
> I felt hurt when you told me to "drop it."
> I felt embarrassed then and afraid of how your parents view me.
> I felt disappointed when it looked like you acquiesced to your father.

## Larry and Acting-Out Behavior

Larry is a coach of a college basketball team. His team has had a successful season, but, as the school term ends, he knows he may lose his position. Students and administrators alike respect his coaching, but they at times are stunned by his angry outbursts. The last incident left his students startled and confused. He stalked into his office, tossed a clipboard across the room, and slammed the door shut. One student remarked, "Lots of coaches get angry, but we don't even know what he's angry about. He just goes berserk and stomps off." Anger doesn't have to be destructive, but Larry's is. Instead of surrendering to his rage, Larry, for his sake and for his students, has to learn to manage his anger. The act of putting words on his feelings and his reasons for them is a first step to responsible self-control. Maybe some of the coach's feelings have nothing to do with the players. Lacking awareness of his emotions and allowing them to fester, Larry resembles a fuse ready to blow at the next provocation. If Larry is to control his outbursts, he will need to heighten awareness of his feelings and to release them sensibly as they arise.

### Reflective Process

First, Larry will need to know what he is feeling before these emotions fester into rage:
Annoyance at his wife for a comment she made.
Impatience with his auto about a recurring knocking sound.
Anxiety regarding pains in his chest.
Irritation at several players for seeming to be horsing around at practice.

### Productive Expression

Then Larry can express them directly:
To his wife—I felt annoyed when you made that remark.
To himself—I feel frustrated with this car. I have to resolve the problem or replace the car.
To his doctor—I feel anxious when I feel this pain in my chest after I eat.
To his players—You three, I'm disappointed in your attitude. Run ten laps, then come to my office and tell me you want to practice seriously.

Larry had developed a habit of bundling all of his feelings into one—anger. The only way he knew how to handle the anger was to suppress it until he periodically released it in a volcanic rush. Under pressure of losing his job, Larry was forced to learn new skills for releasing his emotions. To his surprise he learned that he had a great variety of feelings besides anger, and that they could be shared without exploding and without seriously offending. By changing his manner of communicating, Larry can become less volatile, and his relationships with his students, colleagues, and wife less characterized by fear and more by trust.

## Audrey and Compliments

Audrey puts the finishing touches on a room she has decorated for a client. Her client watches her and then tells her, "This is beautiful. You are so good at your work," to which Audrey responds, "Oh, you're sweet. This was very easy. Really, this was nothing." Her client presses her, "No, I mean it. You did a marvelous job. I'm really impressed." Audrey glibly remarks, "You're very kind." Audrey can't take a compliment. Her feelings get in the way, and she brushes off the kind words. Maybe her first step is to learn to say "thank you." Then she can learn to register how her feelings have been preventing her from graciously accepting the gift of a compliment. Audrey can grow to realize that a genuine response to a compliment can facilitate a more authentic and more satisfying encounter.

### Reflective Process

Audrey has to admit to the behaviors she is exhibiting that are not the gracious acceptance of a compliment:
Putting her work down—"This was very easy."
Attributing the compliment to the generosity of her
    client—"You're sweet."

The next step for Audrey is to acknowledge the feelings that a compliment evokes:
Awkwardness with affirmation.
Fear of appearing conceited.
Pleasure at being seen as talented.

### Productive Expression

Finally, Audrey can respond directly:
I am glad to hear your appreciation of my work.
I am pleased that you are happy with my work.
I'll savor your words when I'm having a bad day.

## Examples of Productive Talking

All of us can learn from reflection on unproductive verbal behaviors—what was said poorly and non-authentically, and what changes are necessary to transform them. We can also be inspired by examples of effective communication. The following are a few that impressed us.

### Darius

Shortly after coming home from school one afternoon, Darius, an outgoing eight-year-old, told his mother that "Billy gave me the, uh, . . . I'll put another finger up" and proceeded to lift his index finger in the air. His mother said, "Oh, I'm sorry. What did you say to him?" Darius replied, "I told him, 'I feel sad, Billy. You're not getting better.'"

What an example! Darius didn't internalize his schoolmate's unfriendly behavior. He didn't counterattack. He simply shared his feelings, perceiving rightly that the hostile behavior was Billy's problem, not his. Darius unwittingly embodied the words of Psalm 8, "Out of the mouth of babes hast thou ordained strength . . . that thou might test still the enemy." The rest of us might not be armed with Darius's serene self-assurance, but we can attempt to emulate his wise and rancorless manner of speaking.

### Deborah

Deborah's fourteen-year-old daughter burst into the kitchen to ask, "Mom, can I hitchhike up to the Yale campus with Tiffany?" Her mother looked at her sternly and responded, "I resent you putting me in a position where I have to say 'no' to you." Deborah's response was not a dishonest, permissive "yes," not an argument starting with "no," but a clear expression of a mother who was placed in an unfair position. Deborah must have been accustomed to expressing her feelings to have been so quickly alert

Most children will respond to clear, consistent expectations expressed with trust and respect.

to them. And what a lesson for her daughter: "Make responsible decisions yourself. Don't force me to make them. Don't invite negative responses from me when I want to give all that is good." And what a lesson for those of us striving to be direct and connected to others: Stay centered. Don't react. Be real.

## Catherine

When Catherine decided to return to teaching after a fourteen-year leave raising her three children, she gathered them together. She told them that to pursue this plan she would need to turn over many of the household chores to them. "I've made a list of these chores, including doing the laundry and dishes and vacuuming the house. I am leaving the scheduling and divvying up of tasks to you. I trust you to handle all this responsibly. I will stay out of it. Without your taking over, I couldn't go back to teaching. So I am grateful to you."

We learned of the arrangement that Catherine had with her children over a year after she had inaugurated it. We had been expressing our admiration for her children when Catherine told us about it. What a contrast she and her children are to the families who wage war each morning about getting up and getting ready for school and who conclude the day with battles over shutting down the computer and turning off the lights. Most children will respond to clear, consistent expectations expressed with trust and respect. Otherwise they can easily become addicted to fruitless, interminable resistance.

■  F O R   R E F L E C T I O N  ■

1.  Before you can share with someone, you need to know what you are saying to yourself. Do you recognize your self-talk as unrealistic or negative?

2.  Do you recognize the moments when you are being critical rather than sharing your feelings?

3.  If you are uncomfortable when someone gives you a compliment, do you know why? What do you tend to say when someone affirms you?

# Chapter Sixteen

# *listening*

I can remember in my early grammar school days, a child would ask the teacher a question and the teacher would give a perfectly good answer to a completely different question. A feeling of distress would always strike me. My reaction was, "But you didn't hear him." I felt a sort of childish despair at the lack of communication which was (and is) so common.

–Carl Rogers

## The Need to Talk Is Related to the Need to Listen

Saying openly what you are feeling is cathartic. It releases the pressure and burden that unexpressed emotion can generate. Being transparent also allows you to be known. It is the basis of trust and intimacy. So why don't you share yourself? Why don't you voice what you are feeling and needing and make yourself truly visible to the persons in your life with whom you would like to be close? When we ask this question at our communication

Parents bewail their children's lack of communication yet fail to realize that they might be fostering the reticence to talk by their own inability to listen.

workshops, the answer most frequently given, whether by spouses, professionals, business people, or students, is, "I don't share because I don't think he/she/they would listen." It seems that people would reveal themselves if they trusted that they would be understood. But, fearing that by being transparent they would open themselves to rejection, advice, or misunderstanding, they keep what is within them hidden, sometimes even from themselves. We have noted repeatedly in counseling sessions that for every spouse that doesn't share, there is a partner who doesn't listen. The same holds true for children, for other family members, employees, and friends. Parents bewail their children's lack of communication yet fail to realize that they might be fostering the reticence to talk by their own inability to listen. So if you want others to be open with you, don't nag them; learn to listen.

## Step One: Recognize Non-listening Behaviors

Step one in learning to listen is realizing that you don't. Just as you have developed an array of unproductive verbal behaviors that substitute for transparent candor, you have probably acquired all sorts of non-listening behaviors. Recognizing them and resisting them is essential if you are going to become a good listener. See if you identify some of the following non-listening habits as ones you practice.

### Responding with "Me Too"

Your friend tells you with evident relish of the great buy she made at Macy's. She is hardly finished before you respond, "Oh boy, I found the neatest sweater on an unbelievable sale at Lord & Taylor's. It was over 70 percent off." A colleague at work starts to describe the fantastic vacation he and his family had at Yellowstone National Park. His description triggers your memory,

"We had an awesome time there. We had been at the Grand Canyon first. Have you ever taken a helicopter to the canyon from Las Vegas? If you haven't, you have to do it. It's fantastic." You hear someone talk, are reminded of an experience of your own, and break in with "me too." You did that? Well I did, too. You saw that? Me too. When you identify with the other's story, adding "me too," you take the focus from the speaker and put it on yourself. *You* are the speaker now. *You* are the focus. This switch is the opposite of listening.

> Step one in learning to listen is realizing that you don't.

## Defending

When you speak to defend yourself, you have made yourself the focus of your remarks. When you listen, your focus is the speaker. Your spouse says, "I thought you said you would be available to watch the kids. I have to go over to my mom's house." You could listen to your spouse's frustration, but instead you hear an accusation and jump to your defense: "I never said I'd be home. I've got a million things to do at work. I'm still behind from taking time off work to drive you and the kids to visit your sister. I've got to work to pay for all this."

Suppose your boss complains, "We have got to get ahold of that group in Chicago. We have less than two weeks to get this proposal ready." You could stop and hear the anxiety, the pressure that she is feeling, and her frustration with the Chicago group. You hear instead *about you* and defend, "I have called out there over and over. I've sent them e-mails. I can't drop everything to keep chasing them." Survival is the most basic human instinct and, unless you are alert, you can revert to defense at the first hint of threat. You sense threat to your schedule, to your reputation, or to your job, and you defend.

Verbal self-defense is rarely productive. The one to whom it is addressed doesn't want to hear it. Remember Sarah Palin's notable refrigerator magnet that advises, "Don't explain. Your friends don't need it and your enemies won't believe it." Defensiveness is often annoying, gratuitous at best, and sometimes slightly paranoid.

For the moment, defending regards the speaker as the enemy to be guarded against. Listening, instead, opens oneself to the speaker. Defending holds the speaker at bay, a stance not conducive to connection, and, if the speaker is indeed attacking you, such defensive remarks will only provoke further attacks. Defending yourself verbally is a futile and self-defeating behavior.

### Giving Advice

When you defend yourself, you are not even pretending to listen. When you are giving advice, you can fool yourself into thinking that you actually are listening. After all, don't you have to listen so that you can offer pertinent suggestions? Not really. When you are intent on providing answers, your focus is primarily on your solutions. You listen enough to identify the "problem" before readying your answer to it. So you home in on the problem and on your solution. But people are not problems awaiting solutions. They are individuals hoping to be heard.

*People usually don't talk to get advice. They talk to be understood.*

Your partner shares, "My supplier is driving me crazy. He's late with deliveries and then he's impossible to contact." You are happy to advise your partner, "Why don't you put him on notice—one more late delivery and he's toast." Your partner doesn't seem receptive to your solution and says, "I've tried that already. It got better for a while, but it's back to business as usual." Ah, more advice is necessary, so you counsel with a lesson, "You've got to mean it." You encounter more resistance from your partner: "I did mean it!" You assume that more persuasive advice is called for so you offer, "Tell him one more time and you will get another supplier. Period." This time you get an exasperated reaction to your non-listening behavior of giving advice. "This guy is the best and the most reasonable in cost. I'll figure it out."

You, the advice giver, are hurt and frustrated. Your help has been rejected and it feels as though *you* have been also. Your partner probably wishes he hadn't spoken. He is still "driven crazy" by his supplier and senses tension now between himself and you, his friend. He wanted to vent his frustration and receive some understanding support. Instead, he got enmeshed in warding off unsolicited suggestions. You as advice giver might be inclined to complain, "If he didn't want my help why did he talk about his problem in the first place?" The complaint points to your unproductive habit of giving advice. People usually don't talk to get advice. They talk to be understood.

"Me too," defending, and giving advice are only a few of the many forms of non-listening. See if you are guilty of the following habits:

### Interrupting

Perhaps you sense where someone is going in the conversation so you cut in to finish the thought. Or you interrupt because you have decided you don't need to hear the rest. You might break in when the other is talking because you just thought of something you want to say. You might just interrupt to clarify (or defend) a fact and miss the central meaning of the speaker's words.

When you interrupt someone who is talking, probably you are acting out of impatience. Certainly you display a lack of discipline, particularly if you want to listen. The behavior can be annoying and sometimes hurtful. By interrupting you might disrupt the speaker's train of thought and, worse, demonstrate lack of respect.

### Being Distracted

Your mind wanders and you begin to think of something other than the speaker's words. Something or someone draws your attention away from the speaker. You are multi-tasking. Some of your attention is on the speaker and some is on the television. Or, one eye is watching the person talking, one is watching the computer screen. You think that you can do it all and listen, too. Check out that notion with the speaker.

Paying attention to someone is a gift to the person. Sometimes you might only half-heartedly want to offer the gift of your focus and so you are readily distracted. At other times you reveal your reluctance to give full attention by trying to do something else at the same time. Perhaps you want to listen but not at the moment. If you are not ready to listen, don't pretend to listen; admit that you're not fully present. "I want to pay attention, but I need to finish this task. Can what you want to share with me wait for five minutes (or until I have finished, or until after the game)?" When you choose to listen, make sure that you really do listen.

## Thinking of Your Response

Do you have this distracting habit? While someone talks, you are busy preparing what you want to say. You pay some attention to the one speaking, but your primary focus is on your response. It is arduous to keep your own thoughts and feelings clear while you try to listen carefully to someone talking. Acknowledge the difficulty, and ward off the temptation to attend to your own thoughts at the cost of listening to the ideas of another. You might have to register to yourself the thoughts and feelings you are having, then tuck them away until later so that you can continue to listen.

## Encouraging

We all occasionally appreciate words of encouragement. The assurance, "I know you can do it," can boost your sagging spirits when you are not so sure that you can. But when you want to be understood, another person's encouraging words can be irritating to you. For instance, you start to share your feelings of concern about your new job, and your friend is quick to encourage you, "You are so good at what you do. You'll be fine." Your own competence might not really be your concern. You might be troubled that you now see your boss differently and less favorably than you did in the interview, or you could be shocked at the low state of the company's morale. Your friend would have learned this if he had listened before offering the encouraging words. As it is, his words in this instance sound irrelevant and even indicate a lack of genuine interest. Remarks such as, "Oh, I wouldn't worry," or, "Everything will turn out fine," can cut off the person trying to share and can even seem dismissive. Listening requires effort; encouraging words are easier and can be perceived as being too facile. Encourage the person talking by giving your attention. Empathy encourages far more than simplistic, even well-intended nosegays do.

### Agreeing and Disagreeing

Agreement can be no more an expression of understanding than disagreement is. You can concur with the opinion that someone is expressing. She says, "I think that the school day should be longer." You agree, saying, "I think so, too, if our children are going to advance in math and science." Or you disagree, "I don't agree. I think children need time outside of the organized classroom to learn on their own." You have assented to or opposed the content of the speaker's statement. You haven't stopped to listen to the reasons for her opinion, and you haven't listened to the feelings that prompted her view. You have focused on you and your opinion. In order to listen in a way that invites the speaker to explicate her views and to reveal her feelings, you would have to hold back your tendency to agree or disagree. Then you would give your full attention to the speaker and listen.

*How* you would listen is our next topic. But remember, unless you identify the ways that you don't listen and attempt to resist them, those habits will prevail, interfering with effective listening habits.

## Step Two: Focus on the Speaker

When you share yourself, you indicate that you are revealing yourself by starting with the pronoun "I." If you intend to listen, you need to direct your attention not to yourself but to another. And just as you focused on your feelings and the reason for your feelings when you were making yourself visible, you focus on the other's feelings and the reason for the feelings when you are attempting to understand him or her.

Your teenage daughter tells you, "The kids this year are totally mean. They get a kick out of hurting people." You turn your attention to your daughter; your eyes are fixed on her. You could ask, "Which kids?" but then you would be fixing your attention on "kids," not on your daughter. So you restrain your curiosity and maintain your focus on her. You give her room to talk by looking at her with interest or by asking something like, "What happened?" She continues, "They were all over this shy new kid about her clothes. They kept at it till she left the cafeteria. I knew she was crying." You could ask, "What is the girl's name?" but you would be misplacing your attention onto the girl instead of your daughter. You listen for your daughter's feelings and say, "That must have been painful to watch." She responds, "I felt so bad for her, but I just sat there." You note your daughter's compassion, but you also hear her feelings about not trying to stop the bullying or possibly not going to console the shy girl. You offer what you have heard: "It sounds like you're uneasy about not doing anything for the new girl while it was going on." Your daughter shares more, "I should have told them to stop." You could try to encourage her, but you resist and continue to listen, "Not an easy position to be in, is it? You feel guilty?" She answers, "I do. I don't think they would have cut it out, but I would have felt better. Maybe then that girl wouldn't feel we are all against her." You offer once again, "Sounds like it really bothered you that the girl could have felt alone, and you wish you had supported her in some way." Your daughter is getting space from you to articulate her feelings without having to fend off your comments.

After she has concluded, you could share your own feelings that have been brought on by your daughter's sharing. "I respect you for your care for the new girl. I hope that you can find some way to let her know how you felt." Your attention and understanding are gifts to your daughter. They communicate your love and let her know that she is completely worthy of your undivided attention. You assure her in that moment that, whatever she experiences, you are there to listen.

## Step Three: Paraphrase

If you intend to improve your listening skills and to communicate heartfelt interest and respect, you must first pay attention to the speaker's feelings and the reason for the feelings. When you have paid close attention and the speaker seems finished, then offer back what you have heard in your own words. In the example we described earlier:

1. The parent hears how <u>painful</u> it must have been for his daughter to witness the scene in the cafeteria.

2. Then he hears his daughter's <u>uneasiness</u> at not speaking up.

3. He hears his daughter's <u>compassion</u> for someone who she believes has been hurt.

4. He continues to listen and learns of his daughter's <u>guilt</u> at possibly allowing the girl to think that no one was on her side.

The father tactfully lets the daughter know that he understands by offering back to her what he thinks he is hearing—her feelings of pain, unease, compassion, and guilt. When you listen, as you offer back to the speaker what you have heard, let your voice rise slightly to indicate that you are confirming that what you heard is what the speaker intended. You are *not* informing the other what he or she has said. You are letting the speaker know what you think you heard and understood and checking to see if your understanding is accurate.

If you want to be an effective listener, you need to have empathy; try to use your imagination to picture yourself into the world the speaker is describing and try to feel what she was experiencing. The father in the preceding interaction imagines himself in the cafeteria, seeing the scene of girls teasing cruelly and feeling for his daughter's compassion and then her guilt. Empathy allows you to put yourself in someone else's shoes, trying to experience the moment as the speaker did. When you empathize, you do not presume to have understood in the manner of "me too" or "I felt the same way" reactions. You attempt to "brush up against" the speaker's feelings. Unless you can enter the speaker's world in this way, you will not be able to fully understand, let alone be able to communicate that you do.

## Step Four: Know Your Own Feelings

In order to understand another person's feelings, you have to know your own. How could you tune into a friend's anxiety, a child's excitement, or a colleague's disappointment if you have not registered these emotions within yourself? The more you have experienced a full range of emotions, the more qualified you are to understand those of a fellow human being. Ralph

Waldo Emerson challenged the divinity students at Harvard to listen well to their parishioners.

> Let their timid aspirations find in you a friend; let their tangled instincts be genially tempted out in your atmosphere, let their doubts know that you have doubted, and their wonder feel that you have wondered.

There are no short cuts to meaningful personal connection. You have to be open to the mysterious world of your own emotions to comprehend another's. Your feelings will hinder your attempts to listen if you are not alert to them. When your child tells you something that fills you with anxiety, that emotion will prompt a reaction from you that tries to stem your fear rather than to focus your attention on his feelings. The emotions elicited in you by your partner's disclosure can trigger your defense or attack unless you grasp hold of these feelings. Hold them for the moment and then attempt to listen. Listening requires discipline. You have to learn to identify your feelings and resist your temptation to act out of them. At times, really listening can test all of your resolve.

Yet the effort put toward listening can be rewarded by an enriched understanding of the people in your life who want to know you and be understood by you. Your non-judging empathy offers them a safe place to reveal their feelings to themselves and to you. You hope that your partner, child, friend, and relative will be open with you. You need them to be. If you listen, you invite them to speak openly. If you don't, you deprive yourself and them of satisfying, life-giving communication.

To reflect more thoroughly on the skill of listening, we recommend you read our book, *Are You Really Listening?: Keys to Successful Communication*.

■ FOR REFLECTION ■

1. *Do you know what you do instead of really listening?*

2. *What makes it difficult for you to listen?*

3. *Can you recall a recent time when someone truly listened and understood you? Can you describe how you felt to be really heard?*

# Chapter Seventeen

# *concluding thoughts*

Try to see it my way,

Do I have to keep on talking till I can't go on?

While you see it your way,

Run the risk of knowing that our love may soon
be gone.

We can work it out.

—John Lennon and Paul McCartney

We need to talk like we need to breathe. Breathing keeps us alive; talking keeps us sane, keeps us connected, and keeps being alive worthwhile. We need to talk to release tension. The person who can't find employment or who is returning from military service needs to talk or risks isolating him- or herself in depression or exploding in pent-up fury. The bereaved spouse has to talk about his grief, the stressed student about her anxieties, the patient about his health. By talking we cope with emotions and experiences that seem intolerable. We keep it together by getting it out.

Talking bridges the distance that separates us from others. We need to talk to get close to our spouse, our child, our coworker, our friend. Often we talk for the simple connection we gain by chatting with the person next to us in line, on a plane, or on a park bench. Sometimes we talk to resolve differences or to reach understanding with someone we work with or someone at home. We connect by talking, not by brooding silence and not by ranting, blaming, or judging. To connect effectively, we have to talk constructively, and that takes practice as well as goodwill. We have to break our bad habits of poor communication and replace them with skills that enable us to say what we mean and mean what we say.

> By talking we cope with emotions and experiences that seem intolerable. We keep it together by getting it out.

We need to talk to unite in understanding with people who see the world differently than we do. Muslim and Jew need to talk; so do conservative and liberal, whites and people of color, old and young, male and female. As John Lennon and Paul McCartney note poignantly, "We can work it out." We can work out so many misunderstandings if we will talk, if we will try to see the other's point of view, and if we will express our own not as *the* way but simply as *our* way. We need to talk respectfully, not with scorn or sarcasm or righteousness. We need to talk honestly—sometimes with courage, sometimes gently, sometimes with tact. We need to talk in a manner that creates trust. Trust frees the other person to talk to us, as well as to listen to what we have to say. Studies reveal that the happiest countries are not the ones whose citizens earn the most income or spend the most money, but are the ones whose people trust the most. The same is true for families, for corporations, for teams, and for groups of all kinds. Honest, respectful discussion relies on trust and at the same time fosters it.

You can make yourself and your world happier by learning to talk more constructively. You can learn to express your feelings instead of judging or acting them out aggressively. You can learn to state your needs rather than deliver threats and ultimatums. You must embrace, as a value and as a commitment, speaking responsibly with the intention of being truthful. When you speak your truth, admitting what you feel, think, and believe, you offer yourself. That is why genuine self-expression is an act of love. Instead of hiding yourself behind silence or words used simply to please or to "fit in," when you say what is really within your heart and mind, you are giving yourself. In doing so, you invite the person to whom you are talking to do the same. Self-revelation creates trust and invites self-revelation. You have a right and a need to talk. We the authors thank you for listening to us. Now we invite you to speak your truth.

# *appendix*

adventurous
affectionate
afraid
agitated
alarmed
alert
alive
aloof
amazed
amused
angry
anguished
annoyed
anxious
apathetic
appreciative
aroused
ashamed
astonished
bewildered
bitter
blasé
blissful
bored
broken-hearted
buoyant
calm
carefree
cautious
cheerful
choked up
close
cold
comfortable

compassionate
complacent
composed
concerned
confident
confused
contemptuous
contented
cool
cooperative
courageous
cross
curious
deferential
defiant
dejected
delighted
dependent
depressed
despairing
despondent
detached
determined
disappointed
discouraged
disgruntled
disgusted
disheartened
dishonest
dismayed
dissatisfied
distant
distressed
disturbed

downcast
eager
ecstatic
edgy
effervescent
elated
electrified
embarrassed
embittered
encouraged
engrossed
enraged
enthusiastic
envious
estranged
evasive
exalted
exasperated
excited
exhilarated
expansive
exuberant
fascinated
fearful
fidgety
firm
forlorn
free
friendly
frightened
frisky
frustrated
furious
giddy

gloomy
good-humored
grateful
gratified
grieved
grumpy
guilty
gutless
happy
hard
heavy
helpful
helpless
hesitant
hopeful
hopeless
horrible
horrified
hostile
hot
humble
humdrum
hurt
immobilized
impatient
inadequate
independent
indifferent
infuriated
inquisitive
insecure
insensitive
inspired
intense
interested
intrigued
invigorated
involved
irate

irritated
jealous
jittery
joyful
jubilant
lonely
loving
mad
mean
melancholy
mellow
merry
mirthful
miserable
mixed-up
moved
open
optimistic
overwhelmed
panicky
paralyzed
peaceful
pessimistic
pleased
powerless
proud
puzzled
radiant
rancorous
rapturous
relieved
reluctant
repelled
resentful
respectful
restless
sad
satisfied
scared

secure
seductive
self-assured
sensitive
shaky
shocked
silly
skeptical
soft
sorry
sour
spiritless
startled
stimulated
submissive
suspicious
talkative
tense
terrified
thankful
thrilled
timid
torn
tranquil
troubled
trusting
uncomfortable
uneasy
unhappy
upset
uptight
warm
weepy
wide-awake
withdrawn
woeful
worried
wretched

# bibliography

Ayckbourn, Alan. *The Norman Conquests*. New York: Grove Press, 1994.

Baldwin, James. *The Fire Next Time*. New York: Dial, 1964.

Balz, Dan, and Haynes Johnson. *The Battle for America 2008: The Story of an Extraordinary Election*. New York: Viking, 2009.

Barry, Sebastian. *Annie Dunne*. New York: Viking, 2002.

Bonhoeffer, Dietrich. *The Cost of Discipleship*. New York: MacMillan, 1963.

Browning, Elizabeth Barrett. *Sonnets from the Portuguese and Other Love Poems*. New York: Doubleday, 1990.

Buber, Martin. "Distance and Relation." Translated by Ronald Gregor Smith. *The Hibbert Journal* 49 (January 1951).

———. *I and Thou*. New York: Scribner, 1970.

Buckley, Christopher. *Losing Mum and Pup: A Memoir*. New York: Twelve, 2009.

Burris, John L., and Catherine Whitney. *Blue vs. Black*. New York: St. Martin's Press, 1999.

Casals, Pablo. *Joys and Sorrows: Reflections by Pablo Casals*. New York: Simon and Schuster, 1970.

Cervantes, Miguel de. *Don Quixote*. New York: Penguin, 2003.

Christakis, Nicholas A., and James H. Fowler. "The Spread of Obesity in a Large Social Network Over 32 Years." *New England Journal of Medicine* 357, no. 4 (July 26, 2007).

Churchill, Winston. *The Second World War: Vol. 3, The Grand Alliance*. Boston: Houghton Mifflin, 1950.

Cummings, E. E. "somewhere i have never traveled." *ViVa*. New York: Liveright, 1997.

Daly, Michael. *The Book of Mychal: The Surprising Life and Heroic Death of Father Mychal Judge*. New York: St. Martin's Press, 2008.

Drape, Joe. "Mine That Bird Uses Shortest Route to Win Derby." *New York Times*, May 3, 2009.

Emerson, Ralph Waldo. "Address to the Harvard Divinity School, July 15, 1838." *The Selected Writings of Ralph Waldo Emerson*. New York: Random House, 1940.

———. "Friendship." *Essays: First Series*, 1841.

Gellman, Marc, and Richard M. Smith. "Marathon Men." *Golf Digest*, November 2005.

Goodwin, Doris Kearns. *No Ordinary Time: Franklin and Eleanor Roosevelt: The Home Front in World War II*. New York: Simon and Schuster, 1994.

Haney, Craig. "Mental Health Issues in Long-Term Solitary and 'Supermax' Confinement." *Crime and Delinquency* 49 (2003).

Hosseini, Khaled. *The Kite Runner*. New York: Riverhead Books, 2003.

Jourard, Sidney. *The Transparent Self*. London: Van Nostrand and Company, 1964.

Kirn, Walter. "What's a Depression, Daddy?" *New York Times Magazine*, November 9, 2008.

Kot, Greg. "Bono: We Need to Talk." *Chicago Tribune*, May 22, 2005.

Lager, Fred. *Ben & Jerry's: The Inside Scoop: How Two Real Guys Built a Business with a Social Conscience and a Sense of Humor*. New York: Crown Publishers, 1994.

Lakoff, George. *Women, Fire and Dangerous Things*. Chicago: University of Chicago Press, 1987.

Lawson, Mary. *Crow Lake*. New York: Dial Press, 2002.

McCourt, Frank. *Teacher Man: A Memoir*. New York: Scribner, 2005.

Nietzsche, Friedrich. *Beyond Good and Evil*. Radford, VA: Wilder Publications, 2008.

Proust, Marcel. *Remembrance of Things Past*, Vol. 2: *The Sweet Cheat Gone*. Translated by C. K. Scott Moncrieff. New York: Random House, 1930.

Richards, Mary Carolyn. *Centering*. Middleton, CT: Wesleyan University Press, 1962.

Rogers, Carl. "Some Elements of Effective Interpersonal Communication." Lecture, California Institute of Technology, Pasadena, CA, November 9, 1964.

Satir, Virginia. *The New Peoplemaking*. Mountainview, CA: Science and Behavior Books, 1988.

Shakespeare, William. *Hamlet*.

————. *The Merchant of Venice*.

Stafford, Francis. *California Catholic Daily*, January 2009.

Stahl, Lesley. "Eyewitness: How Accurate is Visual Memory?" *60 Minutes*, March 8, 2009.

Tillich, Paul. *The Courage to Be*. New Haven, CT: Yale University Press, 1952.

Toibin, Colm. *The Heather Blazing*. New York: Penguin Books, 1993.

Waal, Frans de. *The Age of Empathy*. New York: Harmony Books, 2009.

Paul J. Donoghue, PhD, and Mary E. Siegel, PhD, are psychologists in private practice in Stamford, Connecticut. They are also consultants to corporations and organizations in the United States, Canada, and Europe. Their work has been featured on the *Today Show*, CNBC, *Good Day New York*, and in the *New York Times*. They are the best-selling authors of *Sick and Tired of Feeling Sick and Tired* and have coauthored more than fifty magazine and journal articles on issues related to chronic illness, communication skills, and family dynamics. Visit their website at: www.donoghueandsiegel.com.